D1590500

Christ's Counsel to His Languishing Church of Sardis

or

The Dying or Decaying Christian
With the Means and Helps of
His Recovery and Strengthening

by

Obadiah Sedgwick, B.D.
Late preacher to the inhabitants of
St. Mildred's Breadstreet,
London

Soli Deo Gloria Publications
. . . for instruction in righteousness . . .

Soli Deo Gloria Publications
P.O. Box 451, Morgan, PA 15064
(412) 221-1901/FAX 221-1902

*

*Christ's Counsel to His Languishing Church of Sardis,
or, The Dying or Decaying Christian, with the means
and helps of his recovery and strengthening,*
was published in London in 1640.
This Soli Deo Gloria reprint, in
which spelling, grammar, and
formatting changes have
been made, is © 1996
by Don Kistler and
Soli Deo Gloria.

*

ISBN 1–57358–050–3

*

The publisher wishes to thank John Stone
for making this book available for
publishing, and for typing the
original copy so that it
could be edited.

Contents

England's Preservation
(a sermon discovering the only way to
prevent destroying judgments)

The Epistle Dedicatory

To the right Worshipful, Captain Nicholas Crispe Esquire, and Mistress Anne Crispe his pious consort, To Master Samuel Crispe, and Mistress Katharine his virtuous wife, with all the rest of the parishioners, my loving friends, the inhabitants in Saint Mildred's Breadstreet.

My Dear and Worthy Friends,

Saint Bernard, with a very apt phrase, answered a special friend of his, challenging him in the strains of affection thus: "Oh Lord, Thou who knowest and searchest the inmost closets of the heart, that I love my friend, Thou knowest it, and I know it; how much I love him Thou knowest, but I do not know." The same I apply to myself and all of you; if suspecting my affection *to* you because of my departing *from* you, Lord, Thou who knowest all things, Thou knowest that I love them, and I know it; how much you only know, but I cannot express.

You were a people (of all that hitherto I have lived with, and of all that ever I preached unto) of the most general union with yourselves, and of the most liberal and unwearied affection to your minister. The main scruple many times to me was lest divers of you should outstretch your measures.

All the respects which you owed and showed to

v

my ministry, and all the encouragement which you heaped on me, I now the second time publicly acknowledge. And as my thankfulness presents itself to you all, so in special manner to you, much honored Captain and your worthy wife, by whose good opinion and affection I was (through God's mercy) brought unto that place, you have so advanced your favors both to myself and some friends of mine that I most gladly embrace this present occasion of public testimony and acknowledgment; not that it is sufficient to clear all accounts, but only that you may know that kindnesses long since given are never lost in a thankful breast.

My desire for you is that you may be saved, and my desire to you all is that you would seriously answer the many precious and heavenly opportunities of God's grace. It is not only a vanity, but a danger, a danger both extreme and sure to dally with our souls. God has sown much seed by many of His servants among you, and, believe me, He expects a harvest. We cannot answer great means with great sinfulness or little goodness. To whom anything is given, of them something is required (even the man of one talent was made accountable); but to whom much is given, of them much shall be required.

My dear friends, if you are wise, be wise for yourselves; be good indeed. You honor our ministry and provide well for your own eternal good when you go into a holy way. But if you go on in old ways, the sight is incongruous and the account will be sad. When minister's doctrines are very heavenly, and people's conversation are very earthly and sinful, a melting heaven and a hardened earth meet ill. At length let us see our sermons and pains in your lives. We preach and die, and men hear and die. We preach out our health, our strength, our lives. Oh that our hearers would take pity on us and mend their hearts and ways! If we boast that our means are greater than others, we must tremble also to think if our accounts before God should prove worse than others.

Therefore, for your parts, as you have begun so, with all alacrity and industry, continue and persevere. Our life is short, duties many, work daily, and reward sure and enough. An eternity with God should make us good, and keep us doing, and hold us faithful, and make us fruitful. To the everlasting arms of His protection, and to the perpetual influences of His grace and mercy in Christ, He commends you all, who is to you all,

Your much obliged and affectionate friend,

Obadiah Sedgwick

To the Reader

If you expect in this treatise what is curious and branched over with art, spare thine eye any further travel, it is not here: divine doctrines serve rather for the stomach than the palate. In preaching these sermons, I followed Saint Cyprian's direction to Donatus to make choice not of *Diserta*, but *Fortia*. I looked very little at harmony which might take the ear, but most of all at energy which might reach the conscience. I know well that there is a lawful and seasonable use of learning. I am not of his mind who would have preachers study no book but the Bible, only this: ministers (if I mistake not) must confide their auditors, and then and there use their choice learning when and where it may not amaze, but profit when all is summed up. This will be found the most comfortable truth. No preacher is so learned as he who can save souls.

And now, if you please, read the work and receive this counsel from me. Above all, strive for spiritual life (it is your greatest honor to be good), and when you have obtained it take heed of dying. The dead man and the dying Christian are two sad sights. It is woeful either to be a brand falling into hell or a star falling down from heaven. The rising sun is more and more beautiful, but the waning moon is more full of spots and darkness. Though all may not be lost, yet his shipwrecks are high who has lost much in his jewels, and almost all in his comforts. No more but this, keep heavenly things as you would keep heaven itself.

Thine in any spiritual furtherance,

Obadiah Sedgwick

Chapter 1

"Be watchful and strengthen the things which remain, that are ready to die, for I have not found thy works perfect before God. Remember therefore how thou hast received and heard, and hold fast and repent." Revelation 3:2–3

The author of this Book was Jesus Christ; the penman was John the Apostle; the matter of it is generally mysterious; the persons whom it concerns are the seven churches in Asia; but the scope of it extends to all the churches succeeding the Apostles to the end of the world.

Ephesus (the first of these churches) is taxed for apostasy; Smyrna (the second of them) is encouraged to constancy; Pergamos and Thyatira (the third and fourth of them) are charged for permitting some idolatry; Sardis (the fifth of them) is deeply questioned for hypocrisy; Philadelphia (the sixth of them) is commended for fidelity, and Laodicea (the last of them) is condemned for neutrality or indifference.

In this Epistle to Sardis, you have:

1. An inscription:

To whom? Unto the angel of the church in Sardis.

From whom? He who has the seven spirits: Christ, who has a manifold abundance of spiritual gifts and graces in His own disposing, and imparts them by His Spirit.

2. A description of that angel and church, what they were:

In semblance: you have a name that you live, so you boast; and so others imagine that you are furnished with vitals for doctrine and discipline.

In substance: but you are dead; there is no such matter; your gold is but tin and your piety but formality. The powers of truth and grace were extremely fainting and languishing, and, as it were, expiring.

3. A direction for them to do, which is, generally, "be watchful or awake." There is no reformation without diligent and serious consideration.

The direction is also special with regard to:

The matter of it: "strengthen the things which remain, that are ready to die."

The equity of it: "for I have not found your works perfect before God."

The manner of performance of this direction is expressed in two particulars: First, in remembrance of the good truths, or rather of the manner how they once received and heard them, amplified with a special exhortation to hold them fast; and, second, in repentance of all evil, especially of their hypocrisy and languor ("and repent").

The matter is so large which might be insisted on that I do not well know where to pitch. I shall only be able (as reapers do in the full field) to cut down many particulars and leave the binding of them to some more skillful harvest-man. Take them thus:

1. People living under evangelical teaching may yet be but in a decaying and dying condition ("the things that be ready to die").

2. Spiritual things are to be succored and strengthened if once they grow languishing and dying ("strengthen the things that are").

3. The state, though visibly fair to the eyes of men, yet may be really imperfect in the eyes of God ("I have not found your works perfect before God").

4. A right remembrance and retention of original truths is the way to revive a dying Christian, to fetch him again ("Remember therefore. . .").

5. Spiritual decaying requires spiritual repenting ("and repent").

1. I begin with the first of these: People living under evangelical teaching may yet be but in a dying condition. For the opening of this assertion, premise with me these particulars:

PARTICULAR 1. There are three sorts of people who may live under the preaching of the Word:

Some are manifestly profane, who are stark dead; there is neither the substance nor the semblance of any heavenly life in them.

Others are cunningly hypocritical, whose lease of profession seems to live, but whose secret core of corruption convinces that they are dead.

A third sort is such as are vitally good. There is a spiritual life truly implanted in them, and a profession in some measure answerable thereunto. The proposition I understand even of this latter sort, that even these may be in a dying condition.

PARTICULAR 2. This dying disposition properly

consists in a manifest decay of spiritual principles; for when a man is dying in a natural way the vital principles of heat and moisture are notoriously impaired. So when a Christian is dying in a spiritual way, those principles of heavenly life within him are exceedingly sinking, failing, and decaying. There is not that strength, nor that activity, nor that assiduity in the spirit or heart of man as formerly, but he works weakly (like a dying pulse) and with less ability. As a man goes with lame legs, and a sickly body, so he walks with wounded principles and a languishing, pining soul.

PARTICULAR 3. But if you will have the point in a more ample manner, then know that a Christian may be dying partly:

In profession. His very leaves may wither; that visible forwardness of zeal and diligence, that wonted presence of his at the ordinances may admit of an extreme sluggishness and remissness. He may grow a stranger to God.

In conversation. His hand may shrivel and disflourish. That former association of his with the people of God may now be no delight, and profitable discourses of heaven and holiness may now be laid aside. There may now drop no such waters from his fountain and very little good from his society. His candle may burn darkly and with a very imperfect and loosing light.

In affection. That flame of love and sea of desires, and Eden of delight, may like a great fire be reduced to a few coals and cinders. Christ puts the Ephesians in mind of their first love that it was left, Revelation 2:4, though not absolutely for nature, yet eminently for measure. St. Paul upbraided the Galatians for that strange coolness in their affections to his person and ministry, whereas at first their zeal was so forward that their very eyes, Galatians 4:15, were at his service.

In duties which may now be chopped off by intermission: or wrought out with voluntary distractions, either none, or rugged, done with a kind of formality, coldly, chilly, carelessly.

Heretofore no time was too long, no diversion sufficiently excusable, no praying satisfying without lamenting compunctions and groanings of spirit, or without some more fervent violence and wrestling with God.

But now this and other duties are like a pulse hardly felt, words suffice, and almost an *opus operatum* is enough.

In judgment: Formerly the mind and understanding were (like the needle looking to the Polestar), with much admiration and delectation, taken up with the meditations of God and Christ and divine truths and ways. Now vain objects are doted upon; poor, inferior, transitory delights and profits take up the lodging, and so fill the soul that it becomes almost a stranger to holy contemplation and meditations. It has almost lost the relish of the studious thoughts of God, or Christ, or salvation.

In gifts or parts: These, through too much indulgence to carnal ease or affectation of worldly greatness or defect of fit employment, may, like a sharp sword, grow rusty, or, like standing waters in a pool, be almost drawn dry and empty.

But, which is the main and worst of all, the Christian may be dying in his very graces: As the health of man may admit of eclipses, and the very life of man may admit of fawning and fainting, so the very graces in a Christian may be much checked and wounded, and impaired in their ancient degrees and acts—partly through want of exercise, partly by not administering succor and strength unto them by a constant application of the ordinances, partly by harkening unto some sinful temptations.

So that now repentance may become more difficult and unable, and godly sorrow can scarce be discerned for that extreme hardness of heart, and faith can scarce find the way, or make any use of Christ and the promises, but the gates of unbelief seem to possess the soul.

Yes, the fear of God may now not so restrain and awe, and the love of God may not so prevail and excite, as they have done in former times.

QUESTION. But, you will demand, what may be the causes of this dying condition? I conjecture these:

1. *Some deadly corruption which has seized upon their spirits.* If poison gets into the body, it works upon the spirits and so weakens and endangers life.

The people of God sometimes taste poison: they are tampering with unsound doctrines which, as they infect the judgment, so they abate their spiritual principles and abilities. The Apostle was afraid that he had lost his labor, and spent himself in vain to those of Galatia, that they were even leaving their hold in Christ. And what was the cause of it? Surely some false apostles had leavened them with error about circumcision and the observation of the law. When the judgment is corrupted with any error, then truths are not of that power with the soul; and where truth loses its authority, grace will lose in its strength and efficacy.

2. *Some deadly wound is given unto them.* You know that a man may die not only by a draught of poison, but likewise by the cut of a sword, which divides the parts and lets out the blood that carries and preserves the life of man.

There are things which fight against the soul, 1 Peter 2:1, and not only fight against it, but wound it; no, not the soul and conscience only, but likewise our very graces.

Sinning not only proves a troublesome wound to the conscience, but likewise a killing and dying wound to our graces. If anything in the world extinguishes or abates our graces, it is our sinning, which is to graces as water is to the fire. But now even the people of God, many times, hearken to some baser lusts and viler commissions (as you know in David and others); and when sin gets any favor in the judgment or affection, it is like a disease which will not go away without a manifest breach of health and strength. Sin lames our graces.

3. *Some deadly neglect.* If the soul grows negligent, it will quickly grow dying. Inordinate abstinence and neglect of food brings a man quickly into a consumption; so when the people of God, through spiritual pride, grow careless of vital assistance so that they do not keep close to the Word of life, nor to the Sacraments of life, nor to the great principle of life by an earnest and constant communion in prayer,

no marvel if they become dying persons. It is with us, in respect of God, as it is with the plants, in respect of the sun, which live or die, flourish or decay upon their conjunction (if I may so speak) and nearness with its heat.

So our souls, yes, and our graces live by that conjunction which they have with God. If we keep not close and near to Him, but draw off, what do we do but draw off from the principle of our being and conservation?

4. *Inconsiderate toleration of particular evils, and not a timely expurgation of them.* You know that if peccant humors redound in the body, and are not considered and purged out in time, they may, of ordinary distempers, turn into deadly diseases; and so it is with particular corruption (admit they are such as we are pleased favorably to call infirmities) or any other sins. If they are not quickly expelled and reformed, they may bring us near the gates of death. One sin may bring on another, or the same sin may steal unto a strange degree of strength so that a person (unaware) is languished extremely. And whence comes this? Not only from an inconsiderate admission of sins, but also from an untimely correction of sins.

The soul should presently have "medicined" itself with, first, a right apprehension of the greatness of the evil in the beginning; second, speedy humiliation before the Lord; third, fervent supplication for mercy and more strength; and, fourth, resolute reformation and abandoning of it.

But the neglect of these has brought the soul into a spiritual languor, and perhaps into a deep consumption of graces.

5. *Defect of frequent examinations.* Though at our original and first conviction of sin and a sinful condition we are very tender and circumspect, and ever and anon feared, and overlooked our spiritual conditions whereby we found singular additions to our graces, yet, after a while, after Christians have got over the pangs of the first birth and have procured more peace and comfort (as if a gracious soul would thrive of itself), they are generally apt to keep on the course of obedience, but think it superfluous—at least not so necessary often to search and view and examine themselves.

And what now befalls them? Surely two great evils: first, that the state and operation and acts of sin are not as strictly eyed; second, that the state of their graces is not as well-known and guarded against special motions and temptations, whereupon it often falls out that the poor soul is reduced to great straits and leanness. The man cannot pray as heretofore, nor find that love to God and Christ as heretofore, nor have that delight in the ordinances, nor do that good in society, nor receive that profit, nor feel that mournfulness of spirit as heretofore. Why? He allowed and suffered his spiritual state to run on at hazards, and the less searching of heart, the less strength of grace always.

6. *Defect of solemn humiliations in extraordinary fasting and prayer.* Those means which beget our graces are likewise ordained to preserve them; and as the use of singular means confers more power and life to our graces, so a cessation in the use of them proves an exceeding decay unto them. It is as if you should

take away the pillars from the house or the rain from the earth.

Now it is certain that extraordinary times of fasting and prayer have been blessed with power from heaven to make the strongest temptation and corruption to fly; no sin is able to stand before them. And so likewise they have been blessed with an answer of singular enlargement and addition to our spiritual state. Oh, how cheerfully, how tenderly, how much more fully and fruitfully is your soul enabled after those duties rightly performed! But Christians grow stranger to these solemn duties, either totally omitting them or carelessly performing them; and therefore they get not that strength over spiritual corruption, nor that fruitful supply to their graces, and consequently slip into dangerous languishing and decaying.

7. *Inactivity in our places and relations is another cause of spiritual languishing and decaying.* A *lazy* Christian will quickly prove a *dying* Christian. The physicians observe that as too violent exercise overthrows health, so, likewise, too much rest may cause extreme sickness because therein the superfluous humors are not carried or breathed away, and the spirits and natural heat are not stirred up to perform their proper functions.

It is even so with Christians, in respect of their graces: if they let them lie still and dead, they will quickly grow weak and dying. Though their life is implanted by an operation of God's Spirit, yet it is preserved by an operation of our spirit's. Therefore grace is compared to fire which must be stirred up and blown. He who will not use grace will quickly lose it or decay in it.

But Christians, many times, employ not their graces; they do not any good with them; they do not stir up their hearts to believe, to lay hold on God, to call upon Him, to walk before Him; they do not lay out their knowledge, their zeal, their love; and in their particular relations they live together, but do no good together; they meet together, but provoke not one another unto further holiness.

8. *Last, all perturbations or excess in passions cause a languishing.* And therefore they observe in nature that immoderate fear, grief, anger, joy, or agony (which consists of anger and fear) desire or care, all these, or any of these by their immoderation, mix the spirit and natural heat. Consequently, they diminish health and strength. And surely it is so in the spiritual condition: all inordinate affections are the impairers of grace, whether it is desires of the world, or delights in it, or fears of men, or grief for losses, but I cannot now enlarge on these points.

I now come to the application of this point, which shall be, in the first place, to reflect upon our own hearts to see in what condition our spiritual condition is. Are we Sardians, yes or no, either having a name only, but are totally dead, or, if we do live, whether that life of ours has not grown so weak that we are almost dying?

Reasons to move you to search your hearts in this particular are these:

1. Many among you (who profess and have a name, and, I hope, the truth also of grace) do not get on. You do not make progress, nor have you ad-

vanced yourselves in your spiritual condition.

Though the Lord has given you plentiful and rich means, yet what you were many years ago, the same you are now. A man may say of you, as we do of our friends whom we see perhaps once in ten years, that they look and are just as we found and left them then. So many of you, after many years preaching and hearing, are just as you were; you have not attained to any further perfection in holiness.

Now this is an ill symptom, for a staying heart is seldom otherwise then a decaying heart. Though creation is perfect at once, yet it is not so with sanctification. The old saying is, grace is either getting or losing: like a river, either fuller or lesser, or like an oak, growing or dying.

2. Many persons express palpable decaying. All who know them can see and say how strangely they are altered. They are scarcely known now to be Christians but by the judgment of the most favorable charity, who formerly have been very forward even to exemplarity. The judgments of men are so altered with fond opinions, their strictness of conversation is so strangely slacked into that which they themselves were wont to call a licentiousness of walking, there is such a dumbness grown in their families, and with all there is such a chilliness come upon their affections. Oh, where is that former zeal, that love and joy and pity, that brokenness of heart, those flames for Christ, and those desires of strength and assurance and circumspection to please your God?

3. Though we are not dead Christians, yet if we are dying Christians it makes our condition very evil and very sad.

(1) *Very evil*: no man can decay in good but by something that is bad. It is always some sinful evil which makes us to wither in spiritual good.

And then it is a thing very evil in itself. If it is a sin not to thrive in grace, it must be a greater sin to be dying in grace.

And then it occasions much sin, for it would be a wonder to see a man dying in grace and not withal living in sin; however, believe that sin will live more strongly in you by how much more weakly grace lives in you. When natural heat grows low, then diseases multiply and grow high. If that which should keep down sin is kept down by sinning, how exceedingly sinful may you prove?

(2) *Very sad*: the Christian condition is excessively perplexed and prejudiced by it.

There is an extenuation of our chiefest excellencies; our gold is now clipped and washed. Beloved, we have no more real excellencies here on earth than gracious and holy qualities. If the naked soul is worth more than a whole world, what is grace, that which highly elevates and advances the soul? But even our graces (in a decaying condition) are drooping and pining. For a man to have a finger withering is nothing to that as to have his heart consuming. To behold a candle put out, what is that to beholding the sun growing dim?

When graces decay, then that which is as the heart to the members, or as the sun to the earth, or as the soul to the body, a vital spring, decays. What was said about the taking away of the Ark, we may say of diminution in grace. Now the glory is departing from Israel; now your honor is lying in the dust; the less good you grow, the more vile you become. It is as if your fair hand should become leprous or your sun set at noon day.

It is a depression of our heavenly strength. When Samson's hair was off, he was then as other men; he lost his hair and his strength too.

When the fountains are low and roots weak, then the streams prove thin and branches grow almost fruitless, for these are the principles of being, and are of assistance unto them.

Our graces are a kind of springs to our gracious abilities. When we are less good, we shall always do less good and more evil. Your wheels will move slowly and your feet (like those of a sick man) will move staggeringly and wearily. There will be much ado to do a little good. Your services will be like the thin rays of gold which can hardly be discerned for the multitude of ashes and dross.

Now this is a sad thing, when at the most it is the most that a man can do to believe, to grieve for sin, to love God and fear Him, or to pray unto Him; whereas heretofore he was able to believe and rejoice, to mourn and lament.

It puts a damp upon our communion with God. There is a double communion: One is direct, which is our active communion with God; another is reflexive, which is God's gracious communion with us. Now by dying in our spiritual conditions, there arises a cloud and a damp upon this reciprocal communion.

We cannot so behave ourselves to God, and God will not so behave Himself to us, as in former days.

For our communion with God: It will grow more

strange, less confident, and more gainless, smaller for heart, lesser for trust, and least of all for benefit and success.

For God's communion with us: It will be eclipsed both in the effective and assisting part of it, as also in the affective and comforting part of it. He will not give you His hand or His eye as formerly. David found (upon his great decay) not only a cloud in God's face, but also a strangeness in God's Spirit, Psalm 51:12. We, by our notorious decaying, bar ourselves from much help from God, and of all manifesting favor for the present. Desertion is ever the consequent of decaying.

It leaves a vexation and restlessness in the conscience. When we take our leave of grace, we must take our leave of peace and comfort. A dead man (many times) rests in peace, but a dying Christian is never without trouble. The remaining grace serves most to trouble us for our decaying in grace.

Spiritual comfort usually attends us, either upon great sorrows for sin or upon great progress in duties. And spiritual troubles usually follows us, either upon great adventuring in sin or upon great remissions in holiness; for conscience will trouble us as well for losing what is good as for committing what is evil.

It makes a great silence in heaven. The decaying Christian shall either hear of much displeasure from God, or little or no good from Him. The ordinances (to which he now more perfunctorily applies himself) shall either be dumb and speak no encouragement, or bitter and speak no strength or peace.

His prayers (which now are more cold and formal) shall either have no answer, or else the answer is more fear and trouble in spirit. God seems to have no mind to speak unto that man who now has scarcely any mind to speak unto his God.

It brings a strange suspicion of the reality of a spiritual condition. If grace is often put in dispute, then the Christian cannot perceive it to thrive. How much more questionable will it be when the same Christian perceives it to abate and decay (usually it must be more than mere grace), forasmuch as nothing resembles hypocrisy more than to be formal in our duties, and, with it, to be withering in our dispositions. A dying Christian looks very much like a dead hypocrite.

To all these may be added other evils, such as horrid temptations, external miseries, and fears of death, but I may not insist on everything.

QUESTION. But here it is demanded, how may we know whether we are in a dying condition or not?

ANSWER. I know no better way to discern this than by a just comparison of things present with things past, as also by a faithful observation of our own spirits and graces. Thus, then, look first upon your judgment and minding; second, upon your wills and affections; third, upon your hearts and consciences; fourth, upon your worship and services; and, fifth, upon your ways and conversations, so may you discern whether you are dying or not.

1. *For your judgments and minds*: Formerly in these there were strong endeavors to know the truths of God, and to search out the mysteries of salvation,

admirable appreciation of holiness and God's favor, and sweet meditations on the will of God. The mind was eminently taken up with God and Christ and grace and obedience and heaven.

Is it so now, or do not worldly things seem great in our eyes? Are not our minds more for inferior good than for spiritual good? Are not divine studies rare, poor, and transient glancing? Where is that study to know God, or to see His favor in Christ unto you? Where is that reverend regard of the truths of God? Where is that diligence to know the state of your soul? Where is that sweet delight you took once to know Jesus Christ as yours?

2. *For your wills and affections*: Time was that your will was a flexible will—easy to obedience, submissive to the divine will, cheerful in the duties of godliness, much closing with divine promises, ravished with love to Christ, fearful to offend, careful to please, desirous of none more than God, loving kindness, strictly hating all evil, joyful in this alone: that God was your portion. Floods of tears swelled your grief; heavenly delights satisfied your soul; mercies were blessed; threatenings were feared. But instead of these, your will grows weary and surly, hard to be persuaded, often clattering with the divine will, impatient of strict obedience, indifferent to please, slow to hearken to the counsels of God and the mercies of God, and the threats of God are of small efficacy, sin is not so watched and loathed, God alone is not so delightful and sufficient, your heart grows more insensible of sin, and hardly mournful; your delights are less in heavenly things. Ah, now, how are the mighty fallen? How is the no-

ble plant degenerated?

3. *For your hearts and consciences*: Compare them now with what formerly they were. How quick was conscience to direct? How apt was conscience to check? How tender was conscience to offend? How unquiet was conscience till peace was made? How exact was conscience to obey?

Is it so now? You can sin and conscience strikes not. God strikes you, but conscience strikes you not. Conscience strikes you, and you care not. Conscience has grown sleepy and drowsy, almost dead and seared. You can omit duties or perform them carelessly, slip and fall, and nothing, or you reform nothing.

4. *For your worship and service of God*: How precious were the ordinances unto you, how delightful? You would rather have spent a day with them than a hundred days in other employment. What secret impressions made the power of them upon your heart? What grief, what joys, what degrees of persuasion, what expectations of hope, what furtherance unto holy duties, what conflicts with and conquests over sin and temptations? What more serious care and diligence to walk with God.

Oh, why is it, whence is it, that now it is not as once it was? There is not that naturalness as formerly. The Word works not on you as formerly; the Sacrament works not on you as formerly. The Word of threatening reveals wrath and you tremble not. The Word of promise reveals goodness and you love it not; fidelity, and you believe it not. The Sacrament opens the blood of a Savior, and you thirst not; you rejoice not. You have grown dull *under* all and barren *after* all. Your dead heart argues that you are a dying soul.

5. *The same may be said for our conversation and ways*: if they are now dead in respect of sinfulness, or dead in respect of unprofitableness. We have now become as the heath that brings forth nothing, or as the briar which brings forth thorns. We turn all religion into a discourse or censure or dispute. We can eat and drink and talk and sin. How have the shadows of death converted us? How chill and languishing are our graces turned?

Well, seriously consider these things (you who hear me this day) and look to it that you are a dying people. More fearful would your condition be than the condition of others. For, first, you have more enlivening means than any people on the earth. No city like unto you for public offers or private opportunities. You are even exalted unto heaven in the abundance and choice of spiritual helps, and therefore your decaying would have more in the account than other men. The more means of strength and life (accidentally) make dying diseases to be the more deadly.

We cannot but approve your flocking to the Word and service of God in season and out of season, as if you would take the kingdom of heaven by force. If now, under so fair a complexion, you should be in a consumption that the vitals of godliness should slack and pine away in your hearts and private walk, this dissonance would be not only shameful to your profession, but also uncomfortable to your conscience.

Again, another way persons may discern whether

they are dying and decaying is by an observation of the acts or operations of their graces: as if they are faint and more inconstant. You see that the root is less able when but a little fruit appears on the tree, and that the spring is fallen when the streams scarce run, which yet were wont to flow. When graces are scarcely active, or are uneven in their general act, surely there is some spiritual languor in you.

O Christian, your faith does not commit things to God as heretofore, and your love is not so settled on Christ as heretofore, and your patience cannot bear in any measure as heretofore, and your sorrow is dry and your zeal is cooled. If your eye cannot see so well, but grows darker, and your foot cannot go so well, but grows lamer, and your shoulders cannot bear so well, but grow weaker, it is an argument that natural vigor is decayed. The same may be said for our spiritual condition if graces do not exert themselves in a former vigor.

I pray you to observe that graces are given unto us for three ends and uses: (1) to be inclining principles to gracious or holy acts; (2) to be enlarging principles to pious performances; and (3) to be cleansing and opposing principles of sinful corruption.

First, they are inclining principles to gracious acts. The nature of man without grace is like a dead man who has no disposition to walk, but when grace comes into the soul it enlivens and enables and inclines or disposes it unto holy operations, to mind, to will, to desire, to do heavenly works, as you see in Saint Paul. When converted, renewing grace in-

clined him quite to another way, and to other acts—
to pray, to preach Christ.

Now where is that ancient disposition in you
unto good duties? Whence is that wonderful unwillingness and untowardliness of spirit in you? How
does it come to pass that if you serve the Lord, it is,
as if it were, of constraint, there is a kind of averse-
ness and hanging back. You do not mind Him in
any measure, and His Law is not in your heart.

Second, they are enlarging principles: they not
only enable a man to good performances for the
matter, but also for the manner. They make us a
willing people in the day of our offerings, to delight
to do the will of God, and to be glad in going to the
house of the Lord.

But now there is not that relish of godliness;
there is not a delightfulness to serve; there is not
that liberty and alacrity of spirit. You have become a
dull and heavy Christian, as if there were not that
agreement between your heart and holy duties. You
have grown very slothful and careless, and negligent
in your work.

Third, and last, they are cleaning and opposing
principles of corruptions. Therefore they are compared to water which washes out the spots, and to
fire which fetches off the rust. And as our corrupt
flesh is said to lust against the spirit, so the renewed
spirit is said to lust against the flesh; and they are
contrary one to the other—still in opposition and
conflict.

And so the time has been that you have found
that grace humbled and cleansed your heart from
the love of sin, and raised tender fear about it and

singular hatred and opposition of it. Yes, the very thoughts of sin were a heavy burden to you. How often (by reason of the rebellion in nature) have you cried out with Saint Paul, "O wretched man that I am, who shall deliver me?"

Is it thus now? Why is it *not* thus now? Is sin quite subdued, or do you think that grace and sin will ever be at truce? No, but why do you suffer those contemplative evils to lodge in your mind or those delightful imaginations to tickle and entice your affections? No, how dare you tamper with acts which are, if not sinful, yet doubtful, and as like sins as can be, and which occasion sin? Yes, and sins prevail much on you, as pride, vanity, and under all this your heart neither smites you nor restrains you. The time was when you would not have dared to do this for all the world.

QUESTION. But if the case is so (may some tender conscience reply), then I fear my state is not right, for I never had so much ado with a sinful nature all my life as of late days, and if the greater power of sin shows the more weakened state of grace, I am then the person in a dying condition.

ANSWER. To this I answer briefly:

1. You must distinguish between the turbulence of sin and the prevalence of sin. The spiritual condition is not decaying because sin is more molesting and rebelling, but because sin is more prevailing and leading.

2. You must distinguish between sin in conflict and sin in subjection. My grace is weakened when I yield to sin, but it stands in strength when it stands

in defiance and conflict with sin. It argues the violence of sin to break out against grace, and also it argues the potency of grace to keep the soul from serving unruly and boisterous lusts.

3. You must distinguish between sin in temptation and sin in the affection. Even a strong castle may be assaulted, and a stout Christian much tempted. Then the spiritual part is weakened when sin is favored. If as there is much temptation in your sinful flesh, so there is much detestation on your spiritual part, your bow yet abides in strength.

QUESTION. But another Christian replies, "If these signs of decaying are right which you deliver, then surely I am in a dying frame; for heretofore when (as I thought) God looked on me in mercy in quickening me from the dead, I had a very melting heart for sin and a surpassingly zealous love to God and His glory. But now I find no such height, and flames and measures!

ANSWER. To this I answer:

1. You must distinguish between equal sensibleness and equal spiritualness. Upon the early stage of grace, there may be more sensibleness, forasmuch as grace erects itself much in the affections (of whole acts we are more apprehensive, being more near to sense) but upon the advance in grace there may be more spiritualness. Though there may not be such a sensible grief in the affection, yet there may still be a pure loathing of sin and displeasure with ourselves in the will.

2. You must distinguish between passionate expressions and deliberate or judicious expressions. I

confess that heretofore your zeal and love might be more passionate and violent, but now they work upon more pure and mixed grounds, and forever know that it argues that grace to be the more strong which can act its parts with less turbulence and unquietness.

3. You must distinguish between grace generally diffused and particularly employed. At the first all the water ran, as it were, in one channel; grace exerted itself mostly in the humbling part and therefore seemed to be very much, because it was very much employed in a particular. But upon further knowledge of Christian duties, grace diffused its strength to all the acts of holiness. It is not the less because the more improved, only it is the less perceived—as health and strength are when totally diffused over the whole body.

4. You must distinguish between interruption and corruption. Spiritual principles may sometimes be interrupted (like a river which yet is scrambling over the bay) by temptations. The passages are not always so open for operation. The very ineptitude of a man's temper may occasion unequal expressions of the visible act, and yet there may be no weakening and decaying in the spiritual condition, for the invisible frames are sure and full still. The will and desires act as much as ever, though the tongue or hand cannot render it. And, besides this, the work is made up by a secret humbling which is so unavoidably hindered from an open acting.

5. But, last, if upon solid grounds, when we are ourselves, we find a manifest inequality of our present, with our former condition in grace, then coun-

sel is better for you than comfort. And I think no better advice can be prescribed than that of Christ Himself to the Ephesian church, slacking in her first love, "Remember from whence you are fallen, and repent, and do your first works."

If, though, upon perusal of these trials you find yourselves not to be in a dying condition:

Then first bless the arm of the Almighty God, who has given grace, and upheld it.

Beseech Him forever to preserve and increase your spiritual qualities all your days. It is by His goodness that you are good, and of His strength that yet you abide in your strength.

Use all the means you can to keep up your graces, so that you sink not into a dying condition.

Means to Preserve Us from a Dying Condition

Means to preserve us from a dying condition are these:

1. *Be humble.* The high tide quickly ebbs and the highest sun is presently declining. Faith is the champion for our graces, fear the watchman, and humility the nurse. Spiritual pride fills our fancies, but impairs our graces. Now a man thinks he has enough, then he is sure to lose much. If anything keeps us from being low in grace, it is this, that we still grow low and poor in spirit. People with rickets have large heads, but weak feet.

2. *Strive for further perfection in holiness, 2 Peter 3:11.* Most of what we have is but the least of that we want. He who will not strive to be better will be worse. In temporal things we should insist more on our re-

ceipts, and that will make us thankful. In spiritual things we should insist more on our wants, and that will make us fruitful. 2 Peter 1:5: "Add to your faith, virtue, and to virtue knowledge;" verse 6: "and to knowledge temperance;" verse 8: "for if you do these things, they make you that you shall neither be barren nor unfruitful."

3. *Quit all formality in all holy duties; take heed of the first coolings.* Much impiety may hang upon much indifference. A cool spirit is always a losing spirit; he who gives way to do duties in a slight manner will, after awhile, be scarcely able to perform them in any manner. But as the rule was "Do this!", so still keep up your spirit with the duty. Stir up your graces in all duties; put out your heart and strength in holy actions of praying and hearing, and that will keep you alive in grace.

A conscionable and cordial acting of good is blessed not only with a preservation of grace, but likewise with an addition and increase.

4. *Maintain a holy jealousy and fear of decaying.* "Happy is the man that feareth always," said Solomon in Proverbs 28.

Three things arise from this: One is tender watchfulness against all decaying occasions. Another is frequent search and examination of our spirits and state. A third is quick repairing of all failings—all which preserve us from a notorious decaying or dying.

5. *Be prudently serious in Christian society.* Spend not your hour in vain disputes lest, while you study odd notions, in the meantime you lose precious grace.

There are disputes which end only in division,

and there are inquiries which tend to edification. Rather study to make yourself better than to prove another to be bad.

6. *Keep up uprightness, and by all means away with hypocrisy.* Say not that the sin is little, for many a man has died of a little wound; and we all know that the small end of the wedge makes way for the greater. Nor say that it is secret; a man may die of a secret stab as well as of an open wound.

When the children of the Prophets tasted the pottage, they cried out, "Death is in the pot." And so shall we find upon experience that a dying influence goes with every sin.

Therefore take heed of all sinning, especially of those against knowledge and conscience. These are wounding and wasting sins. Tender and upright hearts are living and lively hearts.

7. *I might add that we must apply ourselves to a living Christ, and to living ordinances.* But these proposed rules shall suffice for this time.

QUESTION. But suppose we are in a dying condition. What means do we use now?

1. Find out the special diseases or causes of your decaying, in what grace most, and by what means and ways and acts.

2. Be lowly humbled, that you have so humbled and abased your glory. You should grieve exceedingly that by your great decaying God has been so much dishonored, His Spirit grieved, religion shamed, conscience wounded, and grace impaired.

3. Then use the means prescribed here in the text: "Strengthen the things which remain, that are

ready to die." From this we come to the next proposition.

PROPOSITION. Spiritual things, if languishing and dying, are to be strengthened.

For the understanding of this assertion, premise with me a few particulars:

1. There is a difference between the implantation, the perfection, and the strengthening of holy principles.

The implantation of them is nothing but their free and effectual communication unto a person from God's Holy Spirit. His hand alone sets all these heavenly plants, and from His sole goodness and power are all those stars, those shining and beautiful stars, created in our souls.

Perfecting of holy principles is nothing but a successive addition unto grace received, a rising or sprouting of those plants, a going on from a weaker to a stronger degree.

The strengthening of them differs from both, for it is not a new creation of holy principles, but a restoration of them; and so it differs from grace implanted, and though it is an addition to grace received, yet this addition is not to grace as merely weak, but properly to grace as weakened; and so it differs from the perfecting of holy principles.

2. The strengthening of decaying principles or habits of grace is a spiritual and proportionable reparation of them unto their former liberty, and ability, and efficacy.

It is not a mere sustaining of them in a birth of grace or in a being of life, so that they shall not quite extinguish. When a house is only so kept that it falls not to the ground, this is not sufficient to strengthen it; for graces may be sustained as radical habits when yet they may be pining in their vigor and remitted in their measure and graduals.

But strengthening of grace imports addition as well as sustentation, like recovery which is health in some measure coming and rising again.

Nor is all regaining sufficient unless it is proportionable to the state of grace when it began to decay and sin. When the decayed Christian recovers again to that ancient pitch of heavenly power and inclination, and unto his old liberty of holy acts, whether inward in the mind, will, and affection, or outward in his open and visible duties, then now has he rightly strengthened himself.

It is true, that before he fully recovers that equal pitch, he may be said to strengthen his graces by way of disposition, but punctually by way of habit. The strengthening implies a new equality, as it were, to the latitude of his former condition.

3. There is a threefold strengthening of decaying principles of holiness:

One is by way of authority and plain causality. This strengthening is the work of the Spirit of Christ Jesus; for as He only is life to a dead man, so He only is medicine to a sick soul. His blood is the only comforting medicine to a troubled conscience, and His Spirit is the only strengthening medicine to a decayed Christian. It is He who must set us upon our legs again, and He who must make our withered branches to flourish again.

Now Christ Jesus strengthens the languished

Christian (as I suppose) three ways:

First, by awakening him out of his drowsy and deadly sleep. Those men said to Jonah, "What meanest thou, O sleeper? Arise." So does Jesus Christ awaken the decaying Christian partly by the powerful knockings of the Word, which will not let him rest thus, but charge on him all the wrath of God and the withdrawals of His love if he continues thus.

Partly by some singular afflictions and near corrections, scourging of him in some singular outward mercies so that he may see his spiritual losses in temporal ones.

Partly by his own spirit, clearing the eyes of his understanding to open and reflect and consider on the decayed condition, and also by exciting the conscience bitterly to accuse and judge him for this backsliding and withering with much torment, fear, and shame.

Second, by conferring on him actual and efficacious strength whereby his will resolves to forsake those courses of death and turn back again into the paths of life. And he is also enabled by that helping grace both to bewail its former decaying and also earnestly and constantly to supplicate the throne of grace and mercy for pardon, and for strength to recover.

Third, by a daily infusing (in the use of means) such new measures and degrees of holiness until the decayed Christian recovers his former ability and vigor, shaking off his corruptions, and attaining unto that strength of holy understanding, faith, will, love, desire, fear, care, and obedience as heretofore.

A second is by way of ministry and office. This concerns the pastors of flocks who should consider the state of their sheep, and if they find any to wander, to restore them into the way of truth. If they find any to be weak, to bear them up in their arms with comfort; if any to be pining and decaying, to stir them up by holy proofs and pious counsel and directions for all the ways of a speedy and safe recovery. And many interpreters think this the principal strengthening meant and intended in this place.

A third is by way of personal duty. And so the decaying Christian strengthens himself when being awakened, excited, and assisted by the Spirit of Christ. He applies himself unto, and continues in the use of, all holy and raising means whether private or public, or both, until God again strengthens what He has wrought in him.

This strengthening is partly privative, in the expulsion of those diseases and occasions which have impaired the spiritual condition, and positive, in a continual succoring of the spiritual condition, till it recovers to its ancient degree and station.

QUESTION. But why must the spiritual condition be thus strengthened?

ANSWER. Reasons hereof are many:

1. Spiritual decays are exceeding losses, and therefore are to be repaired and strengthened. They are a loss:

In that which is our excellency. Holiness is the glory of God and the dignity of a Christian. It is holiness which makes you differ from men, more than reason makes you differ from beasts. If with him in the gospel you should lose your sheep, or with her in the gospel, you should lose your coin, you would seek to recover them. How much more when you are losing your crown?

In that which is our safety. Graces are not only beautiful garments, but powerful weapons. You lose your weapons in the very field before your enemies. You lose your spirituals, and make yourself naked, so that any temptation may insult over you and wound you. At least you cannot so well wield and use your weapons. What can a broken arm do, especially with a dull weapon, against strong and skillful adversaries?

In that which is our serenity. The weakened grace and the wounded conscience still go together; or, if not, then it is the dying grace and the dead conscience which is far worse than the other.

In that which is our felicity. Ah, unhappy Christian, who when your bow abides in strength could see a loving God, enjoy a gracious Father, could speak to Him much, and hear from Him much; but now your confidence has changed into fears, your sun into darkness, your communion into strangeness, and your glory into shame.

2. Who knows what the end will be if you strengthen not your decaying graces? The Lord knows how far you may fall if you will not think of rising.

You see how poor a crop of duties comes from your decaying graces. You feel your affections almost gone; you apprehend not only a weakness, but a weariness in holy services; you find your appetite gone from the Word. You know your neglect of many a Sacrament; you cannot but observe a vanity to arise in your mind instead of heavenly purity, and a more delightful consociation with vain and idle persons than with solid and fruitful Christians.

Yes, and since your graces have been weakened, easy temptations have been very likely (if not altogether) effectual to ensnare you to great transgressions. From many omissions you are now ready for great commissions. So that like a stone running down a hill, or a man carried further and further into the sea, you endanger (what in you lies) the very soul and salvation of yourself. And the love of God, is it not setting? Are not His frowns rising?

And here will be work now made for that miserable soul of yours, which has so far gone from home and is departed from your Father's house.

3. We are bound to keep our graces in repair, and more than that we are not to rest in a decaying state, but to recover.

As the tenant who takes a house is bound to keep it in repair, so that it may be habitable against wind and weather, so must we keep up the graces given unto us and not let them sink at all.

No, more than this, we are bound against not only decaying, but against mere standings. We must proceed from faith to faith; we must perfect holiness in the fear of God; we must grow in the love and knowledge of our Lord Jesus; we must abound in all the fruits of righteousness; we must use and increase our talents. It will not be an answer of proof to retain our naked talent and say, "Master, there is Thine own."

Chapter 2

The First Use of Application

The first use of this point shall be to stir us up to the practice of this duty. I will not spend time to demonstrate that we need strengthening. I may speak my conscience with grief that, generally, we are a decaying people in the powers of godliness and flames of holy affections; yes, our own consciences secretly testify against us this day that so it is. Yes, the judgments of God, the fire of His wrath which begins to burn and fly abroad in this city yet again, testifies as much. And therefore my exhortation to us all is that we wisely consider our dying and decaying. Ah, if the plague should break into our dwellings and take us away in our decayed states, a tormenting sore and a tormenting conscience, a dying spirit and a dying body, both at once, the Lord knows the woefulness of such a condition! There are only three things which I shall commend unto you for the application of this: (1) the motives to excite us; (2) the means to perform it; and (3) the manner of doing it.

The Motives to Excite Us

The motives to excite us, to strengthen our spiritual condition, shall be drawn from the disadvantages in a weakened condition and the advantages of a strengthened condition.

In respect of duties. The Christian man is to be God's workman. He is the servant of the Lord, who imposes on him not a few, but many works; not easy, but (many times) difficult works; not for a while, but constant works; such duties that a little knowledge will not serve the turn, nor a little wisdom, nor a little faith, nor a little patience. Some of these duties are active, some passive, some respecting his general, some his particular calling, some of relation to God, some to man, some to himself. Now the weakened Christian is nobody to the strengthened Christian for duties, for every man is as his strength is, and our actions (for the course of them) are as the ability of the soul is from whence they come.

The weakened Christian comes very short of the other, both for:

His adaptation of spirit unto duty. There is not that connaturalness (if I may so speak) of his spirit to spiritual offices; duties come hardly from him, like a rusty key to open a door. He does his work with a more indisposed spirit; not freely, but like a sick man. He goes very little, and is quickly weary, and poorly, not fully. Whereas the strengthened Christian's duties flow from him as from an easy principle, and lively and quick cause.

His equivalency of duty to the rule. He does not mind the rule of holy actions so much, nor does he proportion his works to the commands. God may command much more than he does, for ordinarily the decayed Christian is guilty of many omissions.

He fails woefully oftentimes in passing over the

duty of prayer, reading, or hearing. But the strengthened Christian is for all duties—difficult as well as easy, private as well as public. Though he cannot intensively answer the rule for duty, yet extensively he does. Knowingly and willingly he omits no duty.

His affective cooperation with duty. He does duty, but without such co-working affections, more formally. He does pray and hear perhaps, but it is coldly and sleepily. It is not as if it were his own work, but as if it were some indifferent work. He acts with a careless and indifferent spirit. His eye is not so full on God's glory, nor is his heart so warm in prayer. His coals of fire burn in a cold hearth. He is not lively in living works, but performs spiritual works without much spiritualness.

But the strengthened Christian has workings in his works, or, as in Ezekiel, there was a wheel within a wheel. He serves the Lord with a fervent spirit, and with all his soul. He is exceedingly glad to obey, and is much grieved that he can obey the Lord no better.

Acceptance of duty. The Lord does not look so much upon his offerings as on the duties of a strengthened Christian. It is true that the Lord does not despise the day of small things, even weak services are graciously respected by Him. But when Christians weaken their own operations, they also weaken God's acceptation, for the Lord is pleased differently to answer His servants according to their different dispositions and tempers. Faint seekers have but faint answers, but resolute petitioners get plentiful answers from Him of good.

In respect of the ordinances. Here also the weakened Christian is very short of the strengthened Christian, both:

For preparation unto them. His heart is not put in such a frame to come and converse with God. He will not take that pain before he comes to the Word; he does not by precedent meditations and prayers bring such a receptivity and teachableness of heart to the Word. Nor for the Sacrament: perhaps he comes and thrusts on the work, but retires not himself, examines not himself, humbles not himself, hungers not, thirsts not, nor considers his particular necessities so rightly to dispose his soul for a holy communion with God; but he is more full of carnal indulgence to himself, and studies rather for apologies to excuse his neglect than by preparative duties to fit himself.

For application of them. He stands under the ordinances with more distractions, with less attention, with an unclosing spirit. The Word works not so on his heart, nor his heart on the Word. He stands under the ordinances with a more distracting spirit, left with a more fearing spirit, lest the Lord will find him out for his revoltings, and either he dares not come to the Sacrament or, if he does, he is not able for his life almost to be confident and persuaded of God's love towards him in Christ.

For fructification. He buys not at the market, sucks not, and thrives not by the breasts, nor makes that use of them as the other does. Nor does he improve them so to the benefit of his spiritual condition as the other does. The counsels, commands, exhortations, reproofs, promises are generally to him in his weakened state. As water on the rock, or as the waves to Jonah sleeping in the ship, they have not that authority over his drowsy spirit.

But the strengthened Christian has far more easy passages; the Word and Sacrament have their sweet and facile impressions on his understanding, will, and affections. By discoveries of sin and threatenings, he fears the Lord and hates sin more. By discoveries of goodness and mercy and Christ, his faith *gets* more and his love *rises* more. By discoveries of duties and commands, his cares and desires abound more in him. They are still humbling, or still purging, still raising, or still upholding of him. He is more and more built up and edified in his holy faith; his communions with God are more cordial, and more beneficial. There is still a fuller and sweeter conjunction between his soul and Christ.

In respect of corruptions. These are the very bane and poison and shame of his soul, the sore wounds and impairings. The weakened Christian is found much underfoot, and is more in bondage and less sensible of it. Gray hairs appear more on him; unruly lusts get more head again; and he either hardly feels them or faintly resists them. He has now become as a wounded man over whom every coward can insult.

The strength of tender perception of sin fails, as does the strength of resolute opposition and the strength of frequent conquest, so that his soul is much imbased by lusts. His resistance is either none, or else it is faint or fruitless. He is overborne by the tide more easily, like an unskillful rower or a sick man by a thrust.

But it is otherwise with the strengthened Christian, who now can lead captivity captive. He is mighty in prayer and resolute in defiance. He is generally happy either in making sinful motions to fly or in preserving his soul from yielding unto them; either he is more quiet or less guilty. He is a greater enemy to sin, a surer conqueror, and still a lesser servant.

In respect of conversation. It is true that the Christian must be gold without and gold within. He must be like the heavens: excellent in substance and beautiful in appearance. A good heart is not enough, but also a good life and walking—like a spring which is for common good and not for private. But the weakened Christian in his conversation falls short of the others who are strengthened in many respects:

1. *For strictness.* Though it is a kind of garment, yet it hangs more loosely. And it is like one of the planets: though a star in heaven, sometimes nearer and sometimes more distant from the equinoctial. There is not that exact conscionableness in holy walkings, but a sordid complying many times with the acts and ways of unworthy societies, or at least his graces are outdared and overawed, so that when he should express them for God's glory he is afraid to speak or work.

2. *For profitableness.* Every good man should be like a tree from which one may gather fruit. He is to be a steward of the manifold gifts, not enclosing, but employing them for the benefit of others. His box of ointment should be opened. If you are good, you are bound also to do good; for graces are given not only

to make us good, but also to make us to do good. But it is not thus with the decaying Christian. He, being now fallen into a penurious stock of grace, has almost lost the art and skill of profitableness. His acts seem rather to be those of civility than piety; he may be as facetious, but is not so religious in conversing. His discourses are more censorious and insolent than substantial and edifying. I confess that some Christians cannot so draw out their treasure through a bashfulness of spirit, but he is grown less active because less able; his barrenness is in the cause and not in the instrument.

He may eat and drink with others, but no good comes from him. His lips preserve not knowledge, nor does his communication administer grace to the hearer. From this it follows that God has little or no glory by him; the saints have little or no delight in him; and his conscience has little or no comfort in itself.

3. *For clearness.* His river is not so sweet, but ever and anon it proves salty. His sun, though it runs its course, yet is frequently clouded. So is it with his life: he is not doing good but withal, ever and anon, he is doing some evil. His weakened graces cannot bear him up against strong occasions and temptations. His gold lies much in the ashes, and, like a lame man, he is not only halting in his best motion, but ever and anon, quite down, the snuff gets above his candle.

4. *For delightfulness.* He is almost a stranger to exact Christians, and does not honor them so much as formerly, but secretly fears their company and judgment. He is perhaps more ashamed, or is more

afraid of them. His conscience is yet so apprehensive that he interprets every glance as a secret check of his decaying. It is not so with the strengthened Christian whose graces are high, his carefulness great, his usefulness large, his godliness even, and his great delights are taken up among the best and choicest Christians. He himself still grows better, and others by him.

In respect of consolation. The declining sun creates the longer and darker shadows, and the decaying Christian brings on himself either the sharper terrors or deeper griefs, and his sickbed is full of pains. Neither his own spirit nor God's Spirit speak peace unto him. He who of bad begins to be good may have much tranquillity; but he who of good becomes less good ever becomes more undelightful to God and most unquiet with himself.

The ship which goes out in low ebb falls foulest on the sands; so Christians who ebb in graces shall always flow with sorrows.

But it is otherwise with the strengthened Christian, for rising graces breed stronger comforts and longer ones too. There is not only no troubling accusation, but a most surpassing excusation in conscience. He has a better heart, and shall therefore find a more quiet spirit; for conscience speaks peace answerable to our being more good and doing more good. Alas, it is sad that you should still walk like a Benoni, a child of sorrow, whereas the other Christian lives like a Barnabas, a son of consolation.

In respect of affliction. The weakened Christian, in active graces, is ever most weak in passive duties. Generally he has more crosses and (of himself) less wisdom and strength to bear them because he is grown worse; therefore his afflictions are increased, and, because his abilities are sunk, the afflictions crush and prick him much the more.

Samson, who could easily break through many cords and bars, yet, when weakened, a few Philistines were too hard for him.

He cannot be so patient, nor yet so confident, nor yet so diligent in a suffering condition.

His weakened graces can neither administer strength, nor yet subdue those workings of impatience; so that he is almost sunk and split with calamities. His decayed ship can scarce abide any foul weather.

But when personal sickness and the apprehension of death comes (at which times his conscience is thoroughly wakened), ah, how bitter, how terrible are the thoughts and disputes of his heart at such a time—much like those of him who apprehends his condition not to be good!

Oh, how the pulses of his disturbing and disturbed conscience work! What reflections on his former ways? What comparison of his former flourishing with present decaying? What fear of approaching the Lord? What smart sentences on himself, what sudden and vehement explanations? "Oh, Lord! I would not yet die. I am fallen much from my God. Lord, spare me a little that I may recover my strength (my decaying strength) before I go hence, and shall be no more seen."

It is not so with the strengthened Christian, but as in active duties he is more forward, so in passive duties he is more sufficient. In losses, in crosses, yes, in death itself, he is more submissive and confident. He can (with Job) be as willing to receive evil at the hand of God as good, and not only rejoices in His favors, but in His strokes, and is as ready to go to his Father as to serve God his good Master.

In respect of God's manifestation. The Lord is pleased diversely to manifest Himself to His people, sometimes in admirable motions and suggestions of His Spirit, sometimes in more quick excitations of their spirits, sometimes in singular confirmation of them with assistance for extraordinary works, sometimes by secret impressions of His favor and love upon their consciences, which revives their hearts as wine, and satisfies their souls as with marrow. So David speaks in Psalm 63. But now the weakened Christian darkens this heaven over his head. He has not that comfortable sight of God, that assurance of His favor, that joy of the Holy Ghost; David lost the joy of the Spirit and the voice of gladness. The arm of God is not so revealed in him for doing of good, nor the face of God so open unto him at all.

The strengthened Christian finds it otherwise: he has a better heart and a fairer day. His communion is sweet with the Lord; he still seeks the Lord, and often finds Him and enjoys Him in His power and in His graciousness. The Lord meets him who works righteousness, and remembers him who remembers the Lord in their ways.

Now think on these things (O you fallen and decayed Christian) and rest not in your weakness, but recover and strengthen your spirituals again.

Helps to Fetch and Quicken

Three things I will let fall, which perhaps may fetch and quicken you again:

1. Though you are far sunk, yet you may be raised again.

2. If you rise again, the Lord will graciously pardon your decays.

3. If you will set upon the strengthening work, the Lord will work in you sufficient strength.

1. You may be raised and strengthened again, and that may appear thus unto you:

Repentance is possible for any sins which are committed; and if renewed repentance is possible, then a recovery again is possible, forasmuch as our recovery again consists very much in a renewed repentance.

Yes, and we have examples of weakened Christians being strengthened again. We know that David was exceedingly wounded, but yet recovered. Peter grievously fell, but graciously rose again.

2. If you strengthen your condition, the Lord will mercifully pardon your former decaying. I confess that there may be foregrounds of fear to untangle and depress the spirit of a decayed Christian, for his sins (by which he has decayed) may perhaps be heinous as to the kind and high as to the circumstances, being against knowledge, against the workings of conscience, against the workings of his graces, against the tender love of God in Christ shown to him more than to another; so that his heart may strongly misgive him whether the Lord will ever look upon him more, and accept him into

favor. But this I say: let your decayings be what they will, either for the matter of them, or the causes of them, or the circumstances of them, if you rise again by a renewed repentance, I assure you that the Lord will pardon you and accept you in Christ. Look, as the Lord pardons all the sins of your un-converted condition upon your initial repentance, so He will pardon all the sins of your converted condition upon renewed repentance. Therefore He calls upon backsliding and declining people to re-turn unto Him. And He promises both to heal them, Hosea 14:4, and to love them freely (ibid) which is as much as to pardon them. But see the pardon ex-pressly in Micah 7:18: "Who is a God like unto Thee, that pardoneth iniquity, and passeth by the trans-gression of the remnant of His heritage."

3. If you will set upon the strengthening work, the Lord will work in you sufficient strength for the work. There is a difference between a man in his conversion—there indeed he is without all strength; he can do nothing—and the Christian in his restoration— there is now some living ability in him which can yet do a little, act a little, strive a little, at least in bewailings and desires. Now if you, in any sincere degree, set upon the right and full means of your recovery, the Lord God will come in with His own strength. He will strengthen what He has wrought in you, and will work the will and the deed in you, His own works in you.

The Means to Perform It

What means may a decayed Christian use to recover and strengthen himself again?

I conjecture that the best course is this:

1. *A serious consideration of their condition.* This is the counsel which Christ gave to the church of Ephesus (decaying in her first love), "Remember from whence thou art fallen." Seriously consider, take to heart, peruse and judge over your state, what it was formerly, what it is now, what strength then, what weakness now, how much glory God had then, what dishonor God has now, what good you did then, what evil you do now, what peace in conscience then, what woundings in conscience now, what estimation among the saints then, what strengthening of the hands, and opening of the mouths of the wicked now?

And this is an excellent means to work upon your spirit, or rather to work of your spirit. David considered his ways and turned his feet to God's testimonies.

2. *A deep humiliation which will follow upon this.* You must break through all businesses, pleasures, and impediments, and retire yourself in a more solemn manner (more than once or twice), set yourself before the Lord, and fall down before His footstool with shame and confusion of face, with bitter weeping and lamentations, with sound judging and condemnations of yourself.

Ah, how you should exquisitely afflict your soul that you should be so mad and vile to lose a God, to lose anything of the graces of a God, for a sin's sake or for a world's sake.

That the Lord should show you more love than another and entrust you with grace (the least dram whereof is more precious then all the world) and yet you should decline from the Lord, not answering this trust, not using those talents which have yielded so much profit and comfort being improved, but decay in them and fall behind hand, yes, even under mighty means of strength always continued unto you. These things should cut and grieve and afflict and humble your soul exceedingly.

3. *A solid resolution.* You must, with full purpose of heart, resolve not to rest in your decayed condition, but shake off all the causes and occasions of your decaying.

If any wickedness has gotten into your heart, you must put it far away from your tabernacles; and if the morsels have been sweet, you must cast them out with godly sorrow as bitter as gall and wormwood.

If carelessness and slothfulness of spirit has caused your decaying, you must (with the church in the Canticles) stand no longer upon this: how shall I rise and put on my coat? But rise you must, and get out of your slothful bed, and thrust from you a neglecting and negligent disposition.

Or, if the world has caused your decaying, either in the profits of it and gain, or in the honors of it and respects, or in the friendship of it and acquaintance, you must resolve to bid them all farewell. Think on it, O Christian: what gets he for profit who loses in his graces, or for honor who abases himself in his graces, or for love who loses himself in the favor of his God? Ah, poor soul, you may curse the day that ever you knew what belonged to your drudging in the world, unto your great friends in the world, and your society with such and such persons! At first you conversed with them with a regretting spirit, then with a silent spirit, then with a yielding spirit. Many, many a day you have come home with conscience accusing and smiting you, unto which, had you hearkened, you would have been much preserved. Well, well, if ever you would recover your spiritual strength, you must peremptorily resolve to sever from wicked society; better far to be a poor man and a rich Christian than to thrive any way and be decaying in grace.

4. *An active reformation.* "Remember," said Christ, "from whence thou art fallen, and do thy first works." So say I now, go to your old works again; be trading for your soul; set up prayer again, reading again, hearing again, holy meditation and conference again, and solemn humiliations again; stir up those coals and cinders of grace. There is life yet in you. Oh, act your life. Faith can do something for you: though it cannot see comfort for you, yet it can see help and strength for you. Godly sorrow can mourn a little. Set it to work; perhaps it may quickly rise to a flood upon particular surveys, and so set repentance to work, yes, yes, and all your soul, your mind, your judgment, your memory, your affections to work in all the duties of your general and particular condition.

5. *Ardent supplication.* It is the Lord who must show this power in your weakness. Psalm 86:16: "O turn unto me and have mercy upon me, give Thy strength unto Thy servant." Beseech Him to pity you;

beseech Him to succor and help you, to be your strength and your salvation, to beat down and weaken the sins which have so much weakened you, to crucify your heart to the world, which has so much crucified your heart unto your God, to breathe upon your graces as He did upon the dry bones, to stir up and revive them by His Almighty Spirit, to put His hand of power upon your hand of weakness, as the prophet did upon the kings.

Yes, and never give Him over till then, that though you have been a backsliding child yet He is a gracious Father; though you have been unfruitful, yet He is faithful; though you are weakened, yet He is the everlasting God, the Creator of the ends of the earth who faints not, who can give power to the faint, and to them that have no might He can increase strength.

Yes, and yet there is something of His own in you, though very little, yet something, and that holiness which He once implanted by a mighty hand, He is now as able to revive and strengthen it by His Almighty power.

6. *Careful application.* Now go to the healing and strengthening waters. You have known the ways of God, and His goings in the sanctuary, how He has wrought wonders for the dead. Many a cripple has gotten strength there, and many a disconsolate soul has found comfort there in His Word and in His Sacrament; there has His arm been revealed. David grew (by his great sinning) into great languishing; but the Lord sent Nathan the Prophet unto him, and his faithful dealing was a means of his happy renewing. What we pull down by hearkening to the

voice of sin, that may be built up again by hearkening to the voice of God's Spirit. But then this must you do if ever you would be strengthened:

Strive for a plain and pliable heart which may yield subjection to whatsoever law or course the Lord shall direct you unto by His Word. If the Word offers you a restoring plaster, but you will not apply it, if it prescribes unto you strengthening methods, but you will not follow them, your heart may grow more hardened, but your graces will never be strengthened.

But this strives to yield up your soul in a humble subjection to the heavenly ordinances, that if they say "Forbear," your heart answers, "I will forbear." If they say, "Do," your heart answers, "I desire to do your will." Cooperate with the Word received when it has gotten into your soul and stirred you in any kind, when you perceived any healing virtue gone from Christ by it unto you. Oh, bless the Lord and get home; work it again upon your soul by holy meditation, yes, and yet again by holy petition!

You must even do in this kind as Benhadad's servants did in another: they watched the words which fell from the King of Israel, and improved them. So must you watch what motions the Lord puts into your heart in private and cherish them; watch what impressions the Lord makes upon your spirit by His Word, and not only excite your heart to embrace them, but work them often upon your conscience. This is the way to make your weak spark to grow unto a flame.

7. *Lastly, there must be lively consociation by a natural instinct.* The weaker things cling and wind up them-

selves by the stronger, as the weak ivy upon the strong oak. So you must inwardly and affectionately join yourself with strong and lively Christians who have skill in the ways of grace and walk in them, who are good and know how to do good, who have hearts to pity you, heads to direct you, and arms to bear you up.

You must exceedingly be repaired by their heavenly wisdom in counseling you, kept in by their tender watching over you, put forward by their daily exhortations of you, refreshed by their seasonable comforting of you, and led on by their strict and lively examples; yes, even stirred up by the observation of those blessed experiences which you perceived in them through a careful communion with God, as also much assisted by the success of their prayers for your particular condition.

The Manner of Doing It

Now be pleased to hear a little for the manner, how you are to set upon this strengthening work, and then I will have done with this proposition.

If you find yourself to be a weakened Christian, then set upon your strengthening work:

1. *Presently.* The physician's rule is that we should set upon diseases as soon as diseases set upon us, not trifle away the methods of recovery. Three things must be looked into in time: tides, seasons, and diseases.

If we presently oppose our decaying we shall prevent the deadliness of diseases. Had you opposed your negligent, careless spirit at first, you would not now be bleeding under so many wounds; you would not have stepped down from one sin to another; you would not have gone so desperately from the Lord.

Therefore watch your heart and often examine it, weekly, no, daily; your languishings are by this manner sooner espied and sooner stayed.

Our strengthening will hereby become more easy. It is easier to fetch a man from the brink than from the depth of the channel, and for a physician to cure a distemper than to heal a disease.

There is usually in the first impairings less corruption, and more strength of grace to oppose and subdue it. Believe it, long decayings are more uncomfortable and more difficult for recovery. Therefore, if you fall suddenly, rise quickly. Remember one thing: it is a very dangerous thing to suffer the soul to habituate itself to decaying. Old customs are hardly broken.

2. *Voluntarily.* It is true that, though you decay more and more, yet the Lord may awaken you at length and recover you; but do not put the Lord to it. The physician may perhaps heal a deeply languishing patient, but it will cost the patient dearly and bitterly. Joab got little by not coming to Absalom, for at length he fetched him by setting his corn on fire. If you will not come in of your own accord, I tell you the Lord will fetch you in indeed, but He will send a whirlwind after you as He did Elijah, or a tempest after you as He did Jonah. He will send flames into your conscience, if you will put Him upon compulsory ways.

No, rather peruse your decayings yourself, and arraign yourself and judge yourself and afflict yourself, and hasten to make your peace and recover strength. It argues the better heart to fall unwillingly; but willingly to rise, hereby peace is sooner made, and strength sooner restored.

3. *Prudently.* When a tree is withering you need not pour buckets on every branch; if you water the roots, it is as if you watered all. There is a holy part in recovering our graces again. If you can recover the roots, you have hit the way to renew all. Now there are two radical graces (as it were) that, if they are strengthened, all the rest will come to be strengthened:

<u>Faith</u>. This is a root grace, and this is a strengthening grace. It is of singular power with God, with Christ, and with the Spirit of God. It is that grace which lays hold of, and applies all our strengthening helps, so that it deals at the springs of strength and brings away strength from them.

But this is not all. Faith is no sooner strengthened to lay hold on our strength, but (like those common officials in nature, the stomach, liver, heart, and brain) it imparts this vigor to all the new man. Every grace gets when faith gets. The more a man can believe, the more will that man grieve for sin, the more will he fear to sin, the more he will hate sin, the more will he repent of sin, the more careful will he be to walk before God, the more tender and conscientious will he grow in duties, the more able unto prayer and the ordinances, and the more successful under them.

Therefore, deal prudently for your strengthening. When a house is declining, we do not meddle with every rafter and piece of wood. No, we strengthen the pillars and foundation. Faith is the pillar (as it were) of our graces; strengthen it to more apprehension, application, to more submission to the will of God, to more affiance, to more dependence on God through the blood of Christ, and faith, will both find out your strength and impart it. "I can do all things through Christ that strengthens me."

Love. This is another radical grace: not that it brings forth other graces for their habits, but only that it eggs on other graces to their acts and operations. For as holy love is a most active quality in itself, so it does make the Christian to be most active; it is a doing thing, and makes the person to be doing. Moreover:

There is activity flowing from love. Grace shall never be idle where the love of God is strong. "The love of Christ constrains me," said Saint Paul. It is like the virtuous woman in the last of Proverbs who set all her handmaids to employment. Love will find duty enough, for it is never quiet but in doing the will of God.

There is diligence. It will not set graces to a naked work, but to a diligent work—even carefully and diligently to express their acts, to take all the seasons of holy actings, strictly to oppose and resist corruption, neatly to set out duties, so as God may have most glory.

There is delightfulness. It makes our communion with God pleasant, and the works of piety easy to the soul. And the more delightful and easy any acts are, the more frequently they grow. David, loving the Lord, was glad when they said, "Let us go unto the house of the Lord"; and he had a desire even to dwell and rest there as the birds did, Psalm 84.

Now put all this together and you shall see that if love is strengthened all our spiritual state will be strengthened, for it makes our graces to be active and doing, to be careful and exact in doing, to be delightful and cheerful in doing good and communion with God; and all these are admirable means to raise and strengthen grace. Forasmuch as the more any Christian does, the more he may, by using his spiritual strength, always increases it.

All know that diligence in acting is a thrifty course. "The diligent hand makes rich," said Solomon; so the diligent Christian is the gaining Christian, and that delightful frequency of acting is like the twisting of a cord which comes thereby to be the stronger. No Christian is so able in the habits of grace as he who is conscientiously frequent in the practice or exercise of grace.

4. *Seriously and in good earnest, and not slightly and faintly.* The recovery of a faint soul will never be effected by faint workings. Gentle medicine is improper for tough disease. You fell into your decayed state by remissive operations or acting, and do you think that what was not able to keep up your graces from sinking can now quicken and raise them, being greatly sunk?

If my hands cannot keep a swooning person from falling to the ground, can they lift him up being fallen? Whereas every heavy body, the farther it descends, the heavier it is.

No, no, Christian, you deceive yourself to think

that a few complaints, a few sighs, a few tears, or a prayer (once in a quarter of a year) more earnestly pressed will serve the turn.

I tell you that your wounds are deep and your diseases are strong. You are deeply revolted from the Lord; the very foundations are shaken and battered within your soul.

What talk have you of putting a soft cloth over your stinking and festered wounds of sinful corruptions? You ought to search deeply and cut off the dead flesh, lest the whole be gangrened.

Take my advice: break up the fallow ground, I mean your hollow heart. Search and try it to the utmost. Do not be slight, but by deep and full humiliation and supplication make your peace; not by common, but by extraordinary performances seek to renew yourself.

Your falls have been great and, therefore, your work must not be slight. Great sinning requires grand sorrowing, and low falling requires the more industry for higher rising. Therefore act your strengthening part with all your strength, and, as it were, for your very life. Remember that David was in fasting, and Peter in bitter tears for their falling, and so they rose again.

5. *Thoroughly and to some purpose.* Do not begin a strengthening work, and then either upon the motions of a lazy heart, a fearful heart, or an unbelieving heart, be discouraged and desist. This inconstancy would keep you in an everlasting infirmity. If a patient followed the prescription of the physician for a day or two, but afterwards found that to be somewhat painful and troublesome, he will be

bound no longer, but then falls ill again. So if you set upon the ways of strengthening, and for awhile you keep close to praying and hearing and humbling and reforming, but if you perceive the works to be painful and offensive to your corrupt heart, and too strict to your licentious heart, or the fruits of them to be hopeless to your unbelieving heart (I cannot hold out, all is in vain, or to little purpose), I tell you that you do but play the fool with your soul; you set it forward and backward. This would be to twist and untwist Penelope's thread. You never will get anything by an inconstant and weary spirit.

But this must you do, if you would recover your strength indeed: You must never admit interruptions; you must never break off your renewing work till you have gotten to your former station in grace again.

The work must be a daily work, a constant going on in mourning and praying, till you have gotten your tender conscience again, till you have gotten your broken heart again, till you have gotten your more willingly and cheerfully obedient heart again, till you have recovered your first love, and till you can do your first works again.

It is true, you shall meet with many temptations from Satan, with many contrary suggestions from your own spirit, and with many discouragements from the world. And it is true also that your doings may not at every time be equal or like itself. You may feel your medicine at one time to work better than at another. Sometimes you may do your strengthening work with more strength, sometimes with less; sometimes with more liberty of spirit, sometimes with less; sometimes with more comfort, sometimes with less.

Yet let nothing discourage you or take off your spirit from the work, but follow on to know the Lord and His strength against all temptations, against all suggestions, against all discouragements, against all your own fears and feelings and inequality of operations, yet give not over, but keep up your services still. Retain frequent communion with God still; be begging still for the strength of Jesus Christ to raise you; hear still; use the prescriptions till health comes. You are in the way, and must not rest till you have obtained.

If you break off before you have regained your strength, you will fall back again and lose all your new endeavors for your recovery in grace.

Thus much for the second proposition, I proceed now to the third, of which I can but give a touch, lest I be hindered in the prosecution of the matter in the next verse: "I have not found your works perfect."

The state, though visibly fair to the eyes of men, yet may be really imperfect in the eyes of God. Among the churches, Sardis had a name that it lived, but with God it had not that name and estimation.

We Christians have the judgment of charity, but God has the judgment of infallibility. We look only on the skin and surface of actions, but God looks into the hearts and spirits of persons. We judge of the heart by the actions, but God judges of our states by the heart.

Now the outward acts upon several arguments,

and for several ends and inducements, may be extremely different from the inward habit and disposition. Persons, for their credit's sake, and for their peculiar advantages, may draw out acts naturally good, when yet their spirits stand not right, either for principles or ends of those acts. To that, notwithstanding all their profession, their state may be imperfect before God. Partly for the frame and constitution of soul; partly for the vigor and fullness of acting; and partly for the mixtures in matters of faith or conversation.

But I cannot now enlarge in this singular affection. It may teach us, above all, to look unto our spirituals as they abide in and flow from our hearts and souls, upon which principally the Lord looks. He searches the hearts, and reigns and approves the actings of the heart more than of the hand. And therefore we read, that he had first respect unto Abel, and then unto his offering.

This should also teach us to study God's approbation more than man's. It is not sufficient nor safe that either we alone judge our states to be good, or that men judge them to be so, unless the Lord finds them to be so. Every Christian is that as God judges him to be, and he stands or falls according to this righteous judgment of the all-seeing and all-knowing God. And so I take leave of that verse, and proceed to the next.

Chapter 3

"Remember therefore how thou hast received and heard, and hold fast, and repent." Revelation 3:3

In these words you have the other branches of the Spirit's special directions to the church of Sardis, which are three:

Remembrance: "Remember therefore how thou hast received and heard."

Persistence: "and hold fast."

Renewed repentance: "and repent."

Briefly to open the words: "Remember." Sometimes the word is taken for the act of a particular faculty of the rational soul, which is called by the philosophers, *Reminiscentia*, and then it is the calling back of a thing or object formerly known and laid up in the memory.

Sometimes it is taken for the act of serious consideration appertaining to the judicious faculty of the soul, wherein apprehended truths are well weighed, thoroughly thought on or considered of. In both respects, I conjecture, it may be taken in this place.

"How." Some read that word rather thus: remember, call to mind and consider what you have received and heard, as if it were a word declaring the matter; but rather in this place it imports the manner, and therefore it is well translated "how," noting the manner how Christ taught and prescribed them at the first, and also the manner how they embraced those holy rules of His for doctrine and conversation.

"Thou hast received and heard," that is, assented unto and embraced those truths and directions of Christ where is expressed, first, their ancient subjection or embracing of the doctrine of Christ ("received"), and, second, the means or ways thereof, namely by hearing ("and heard").

I cannot possibly with any profit insist on all the observables out of these and the other words, considering that little part of time which remains for me to work among you. I will only point out three singular propositions:

PROPOSITION 1. Holy truths once received are often to be remembered and thought on ("Remember").

PROPOSITION 2. Acceptance of truths is not enough, but Christians must add thereto a persistence in truths ("hold fast").

PROPOSITION 3. Renewed repentance is required of Christians as well as initial ("and repent").

You see that all these propositions naturally flow from the text, and are very proper for us, and for the occasion upon which they are handled. I begin with the first of them:

PROPOSITION 1. Holy truths once received are often to be remembered and thought on.

There are three things which should fall into a frequent consideration: our former sins, and this will keep us humble; God's former mercies, and this will make us thankful; received truths, and these will make us dutiful and fruitful.

The Jews were to bind them as frontlets between their eyes, Deuteronomy 6:8, to which Solomon alludes in Proverbs 6:21, "bind them continually upon thy heart, and tie them about thy neck," and Ecclesiastes 12:11, "they are to be as nails fastened." Look on David, and this was his practice in Psalm 119, "I will meditate on Thy statutes." Then read verse 23: "Thy servant did meditate in Thy statutes." There is the second time, but then read verse 48: "I will meditate in Thy statutes." There is the third time. What I speak of once, twice, or thrice, see in verse 97: "Oh, how I love Thy law, it is my meditation all the day."

The Apostles are frequent in their exhortations to this purpose, to remember, to lay up, to keep in mind, not to forget the holy doctrines delivered by them, nay, and Christ pressed the same also upon them upon many occasions. But for the clear opening of this proposition, premise with me these particulars.

1. The frequent remembering of former truths must be a remembrance by way of subjection, and not by way of contradiction. We must not remember and question them, much less abuse and pervert them, least of all oppose and despise them.

2. The remembrance must be ingenuous and not prejudicial; though we must stick to, yet not in the truths received, our former remembrance, we must not contract a present or future neglect of any other truths which God shall reveal unto us, as when many remember the sermons of dead men and slight the discoveries of the living.

3. There is a threefold remembrance of former truths:

<u>Notional</u>: Which is like often looking into a glass, or when a person beholds truths as he does pictures, gazes at them, and that is all.

<u>Verbal</u>: When a person renews his acquaintance and compliments with truth only. His memory only loads his tongue, like an astronomer who knows heaven and can only talk of it.

<u>Practical</u>: When the remembrance is like a cloud descending on the plants, or like a fire felt as well as seen. This kind of remembrance has three degrees in it, for it is partly:

Directive: When truths remembered are made a compass for us to sail by, or copies for us to write after, still teaching and guiding us how to draw the lines and letters of our conversation.

Affective: When truths remembered are like the conference of Christ (rising from the dead) burning and enflaming of our hearts with most affectionate love unto them.

Effective: When truths remembered are truths obeyed; we often consider former doctrines, and still better our present conversations.

After this practical form, how are we to remember received truths?

There is:

1. *A material remembrance*, which is partly of the things themselves, partly of the revelation of them, partly of the manner and means of revealing them.

2. *Formal remembrance of truths received*, which is rather of the manner how we received them. We are

often to think on truths received, not only as they stand in proposition or revelation, but also how they stood with us when we received them for energy or operation. Thus I conjecture we are to remember truths received:

We are to remember truths received with regard to what estimations and admirations we received them—like those people who have the sun but half the year. They run after it, and are ready to adore it in its approach. So when we did receive holy truths at the first, we received them as the very oracles of God, not as the words of man, but as they are, indeed, the words of God.

We are to remember truths received with that subjection of spirit with which we received them. We not only admired their excellency, but felt their efficacy. The Word came not in word only, but in power and authority over our very consciences; and this power was a full power and an easy power. The truths which we received commanded and awed and ordered our whole man; and we too were most willing to resign up ourselves to the obedience of the gospel in all things, and to be cast into that mold of heavenly doctrine.

We are to remember truths received with regard to what affections we received them. O then, those conflictings of spirit, Hebrews 10:32, whose baths of grief and heavenly compunction with them, Acts 2:37, those flames of love, with those Christians, Acts 4:32, those raptures of joy with Lydia, Acts 16, yes those extensions of zeal with the Galathians to Saint Paul, Galatians 4, the Word had a surpassing influence upon all our affections to melt and convert, to raise and dispose of them.

We are to remember truths received with regard to that resolute loyalty we had, so that we hated and defied all contrary errors and ways. And so our hearts were sworn to divine truths and, as it were, espoused to them, so that we once resolved to live and die in those truths and for those truths. We could not endure any mixture with them, nor hear of any divorce from them.

We are to remember truths received with regard to what reverence we embraced the ambassadors of heavenly truths. They were as the angels of God to us, and we were like (almost) Cornelius, adoring the Peters and Pauls, I mean the ministers of God revealing His truths unto us. The feet of those who brought unto us the glad tidings of our salvation were beautiful and most acceptable unto us.

Now here are two questions briefly to be resolved.

QUESTION 1. What truths heard and received are we often to consider and remember?

ANSWER. There must be an endeavor to remember all the truths. Christ said of the fragments, "Gather them up, and let none be lost." So it must be said of holy truths (on which the soul hast formerly fed), "Gather them all up, let none be lost." You see that the goldsmith not only looks after the mass of gold, but he carefully looks after every ray and dust of gold and preserves it.

Every truth of God is precious. It is more precious than gold; it is excellent, and as it is excellent in itself so it may be useful to us. There is not a star in heaven but is of some good to the lower world. So there is not one truth of God but may be some good use to a Christian.

But if either for the multitude of truths, the sublimity of truths, for the obscure manner of discovering these truths, for the impotence and irretentiveness of an unholding and unclasping memory, or for the space of time since truths were delivered and received, it so falls out that all heard and once received truths will not stand upon record into which they have been entered, but are in many places defaced and canceled,

There must at least be a faithful remembrance of the most necessary and chief truths, namely of those which more immediately and intimately and unavoidably concern our salvation, of which (for method's sake) I conjecture there may be three heads:

1. That vital truth concerning Christ and faith in Him is the great fundamental truth.

2. That vital truth concerning repentance in the conversion of the heart from dead works.

3. That practical truth concerning obedience in ordering the life and course of a converted person.

As the moralists say of fame, or of a man's good name, "Whatever commodity you lose, be sure to preserve that jewel of a good name." That is, so choose a jewel that whatever a man loses, he must yet take heed and care of that. The same may be said of these forenamed truths: though through some defect or frailty or malignity any other historical or problematical truths may slip from us, yet these must be written in our hearts with the point of a diamond and as in marble. The characters of them are to be kept fresh and alive, and are never to be blotted out.

QUESTION 2. And why must this faithful and frequent remembrance, or renewed consideration of truths be heard and received? The reasons thereof are many.

REASON 1. Though sometimes an assent may be sufficient to a particular word of truth for the present, yet the virtue and use of that may be for the future.

It is with truths as it is with treasuries, where into much gold or silver is put and kept safe: a little whereof may serve for the time being, but most or all of it may be brought out upon future and several occasions.

Or as it is with friends and garments, which though we do not use every one of them everyday; yet ere we die, we may have a useful occasion for them all.

The truths which you have heard from the Word ten years ago may serve you twenty years hence. That discovery of the mercy of God, of the blood of Christ, of the freeness of grace, may be of great avail unto you, and of sweet and proper help unto you when you commence to old age or to a dying bed.

It is not with truths heard and received as with our meat eaten and digested, the virtue of which may be gone in few days, but rather as it is with a lease, for life which this year brings in our revenue, and so it does the next year. So divine truths may yield unto you present comfort and strength, yes, and they can, being rightly embraced, be the staff in your hand tomorrow to support you, and be the river in your conscience to refresh you. That heavenly truth which was your star at this time may fitly, upon occasions, serve to be your guide at any time, as the star to the wise men which appeared the second time.

REASON 2. Frequent remembrance of divine truths is (as it were) a spur to further obedience, and therefore Saint Peter joins putting in remembrance and stirring up, as if we should revive our services when we did renew our memories.

Every truth newly and seriously thought on is, as it were, a second sermon or repetition, an inculcating of it upon our hearts. I am sure it is like a further digestion which serves for the better health and strength of our bodies.

REASON 3. It is a means to greatly strengthen our graces. The philosophers say that we are nourished by that of which we are generated. The truths of God beget our graces, and the same truths well remembered and perused will increase them.

Those promises which heretofore inclined your heart and persuaded it to believe can perpetually bear and raise up your heart to stronger degrees of belief. When Christ would help His disciples against a particular infidelity, He objected unto them, "Why do ye not remember?" intimating that a right remembering of His works would have enabled them much against unbelief.

And so does the remembrance of the words of Christ, of His truths, which are as able to build us up in grace as to communicate it unto us.

REASON 4. It is a revocation from sinning. David

said, "I considered my ways, and turned my feet unto Thy testimonies." The same may be said of holy truths: a remembering consideration of them is a recovering of an erring and falling soul. Saint Peter forgot his Master, and then forgot himself. He forgot the words of a Master, and then forgot the duty of a servant; but Peter recovered himself again. And how did he so? The text says that he remembered the words of Jesus, and when he had thought thereon he went out and wept bitterly.

REASON 5. It is an avocation or withholding from errors. Why do men so commonly slip into new errors? One main cause is that they have let slip old truths; they have lost their touchstone to try doctrine by; they do not remember what and how they have heard and received, and therefore they destroy what they themselves have built.

Like a ship which has lost her anchor, tossed with waves and winds every way, so they are hurried and puffed up and down with every wind of doctrine. But he who rightly remembers the truth has not only thereby a touchstone to try and discover contrary errors, but likewise a buckle to secure his judgment, and a sword to cut off the corrupt reasoning and fallacies of the gainsayer.

REASON 6. Lastly, it is of singular good and concern to a distressed and deserted soul, and to a debarred person.

The days of famine may befall you, and then the food which Joseph laid up may preserve you. If future means should fail, will not former and remembered truths be of comfort? And are you sure that seasons will last forever? Where is Jerusalem, who did not know her day of peace? And where are the seven churches of Asia? Or the days of sickness may befall you, wherein you are debarred of the market, I mean, the public assembly of the saints, and are so weakened that you cannot read at all. If now your soul can remember God, and remember the truths of God, and can secretly confer with them, they may be of blessed help and peace unto you. Yes, the days of desertion may befall you; the Lord may not look on you as formerly. He may not confer at all with you in sense and feeling; and what refuge have you now but to fly to the truths of God, through which you heretofore heard Him and perceived Him, and this may prove a support and solace to your heart.

Sure I am that Asaph in his desertions did so. See him in Psalm 77:10: "I will remember the years of the right hand of the Most High; I will remember the works of the Lord, surely I will remember Thy wonders of old." Former embraces are new encouragements.

Thus for the explication and confirmation of the point, I now come to the application of it to ourselves.

Should received truths be remembered then?

Hearing is not all. Some there are who hear not at all. They are like the deaf adders which refused to hear the voice of the charmer. Christ is pleased to speak, but they are not pleased to hearken. How much have these to answer for? Others hear, and that is all. The Word is but a natural sound to excite that natural faculty of hearing, but they understand not what they hear. The Word preached is as a book sealed up unto them: they think it enough to come to church. Others hear and understand the truths delivered, but then they mind them no more. They leave all at the church door as we do our friends at the grave, forgetting that we came to a feast to carry away, and not to a grave to leave all behind. It is as if the Word were a tale or a dream: it is instantly forgotten. In comes the world, out goes the Word. To secular business or sinful acts they presently apply themselves, and so the Word is squeezed out like water out of a sponge, or the characters of it glide away like the impressions of a seal upon the slippery water.

Perhaps many thousands of sermons they have heard in their days, and would think it a mortal fault not to hear, but for meditating, pondering, reviewing of delivered truths, calling them to mind, the better to order their hearts and lives, they will not trouble themselves so far. As if truth were a burden or an unworthy companion.

Now to the forgetful hearer, I would commend these things to be considered of:

1. If his forgetfulness is only of good things (when yet in any other thing and business his remembrance is quick enough, he can remember a tale or story twenty years since), it is a very uncomfortable sign.

I confess that every good man's memory is not an equal treasury, not perhaps a very fruitful soil, but to have a memory like an utterly barren womb, retentive of no spiritual truths, but like sand in a glass, put in the one part and instantly running out to the other, this total and absolute falseness in our mem-

ories is a shrewd presumption that either we do not
at all rightly conceive of and understand spiritual
truths, or, if we do, we do not much care for them or
respect them.

2. Forgetfulness of truths heard and received is a
kind of very evil ignorance. The schoolmen distinguish between what a man does not know and where
either a man will not know or unfits himself to
know. Thus is it with forgetfulness: truths forgotten
are like truths unknown, and the more that the
knowledge of former truths wear out, the less capac-
ity is there to apprehend and receive further truths.

Nor is this all. Forgetfulness is not only a curtain
drawn over knowledge, but it is a bar also to our
practice. The forgetful hearer can be no good prac-
titioner. For no man acceptably practices more than
he knows, and no man properly knows more than
he remembers.

Nor is that all. Forgetfulness keeps us not only in
a state of ignorance and blindness, nor only in a
state of barrenness and undoingness, but further yet
it keeps us in a condition of sadness and uncom-
fortableness, for all our comforts depend upon divine truths (they are our springs of joy); but with this
caution, so far as they are solidly and rightly applied
by us (as strong waters refresh when they are taken),
now for the forgetting person, there can be no good
using where there is no good remembering of holy
truths.

So that now, by your forgetfulness, divine truths
are lost, and the operations of them are lost; they
can neither guide you nor help you, nor preserve or
comfort you at all. And if all these are lost, you can-

not be safe. Whatsoever opinion you will have of yourself, James 1:22 assures you that you deceived your own self.

3. If remembering truths heard and received is necessary, then be pleased to act the point which Christ here charges: "Remember how thou hast received and heard."

You have perhaps heard of the doctrine of sin and knowledge thereof by the law out of Romans 7:7. You have heard of the manifold aggravations of sin in several texts, as being against knowledge, means of grace, mercies, afflictions, covenants, and of infidelity (that binding sin) out of 1 John 3. You have heard many a sermon of the power of the Word for conviction and conversion, for consolation, for conversation, and for salvation, out of 2 Thessalonians 1.

You have heard of the impediments of the soul from coming to Christ, partly from the love of sin, John 3, partly from the love of the world, Mark 10:22, and partly from the perverseness of our wills, Matthew 23:37.

You have heard much of faith, for the nature of it, out of Acts 16; for the degrees of it, out of Mark 9; for the use of it in all the promises, out of 2 Corinthians 1, and of our love to God, out of Psalm 31:23.

You have heard the doctrine of repentance from dead works largely opened out of Acts 17:30, and further unfolded in the conversion of the Prodigal out of Luke 15, and of the doctrine of temptations out of Luke 4, the kinds of them, and methods of defense and conquest.

You have lately heard of that comfortable, ample, perpetual care and goodness of God's providence over His church and people out of Psalm 23 all over.

Lastly, you have heard something of a languishing, and of a recovering soul from this out of Revelation 3:2.

I call God to record at this day that (according to my knowledge and ability) I have (as Saint Paul, Acts 20:27) "not shunned to declare unto you all the counsel of God requisite to your salvation, testifying unto you all repentance towards God, and faith towards our Lord Jesus Christ," verse 21, yea, in season and out of season, in strength, in weakness, in public, in private have I desired and endeavored your everlasting good.

Now let not these pious truths slip from you, or be as water spilt upon the ground. Ministers die, but let not truths die. Ministers depart, but let not truths depart. Stony hearts are bad, but iron memories are good. If you have heard truths and received them, why, still retain the truths for the truth's sake; let them ever abide with you, live with you, die with you. And do not lock up the truths only, but let your memories faithfully serve out those truths according to your particular occasions and occurrences of your life. Hold them out to keep out errors; bring them out to keep up graces; improve the directions of the Word to lead your ways, and the comforts of the Word to refresh and encourage your hearts, and that you may skill the art of heavenly memory, know that:

Helps to a Holy Memory

There are six things which will much avail to help and enable the remembrance of truths heard and received.

Ardent affection. Love is a safe lock and a ready hand. That which we much like we shall much mind. David was fervent in love, and therefore frequent in thinking of God's law. Psalm 119:97: "Oh how I love Thy law! It is my meditation all the day." Here was great love and great studying; a child will not forget his mother.

Frequent meditation. Many earthly things wear out by handling (as characters in gold or silver), but heavenly characters abide longest where they are most used. Every new and serious contemplation of them makes a fairer and firmer impression. It is like a second stamping of them. The memory is like a glass, and the understanding as an eye looking back into it: the more frequent acquaintance and familiarity that the understanding has, by reflecting on the memory, the more strongly are things engraved in our remembrance.

Constant operation. If memory were more used, memory would be more useful. When you have heard a sermon and are at home, then call your memory to an account. How has it played the faithful steward for you? What truth has it remembered?

By a daily striving to remember, you shall daily perfect the remembrance.

A distinct apprehension. Saul was not easily found in the stuff, and confused minds are seldom linked with exact memories. The more orderly and exact that the understanding is, the more easy is the re-membrance of things. Take heed of ignorant minds that know not truths, and of confused minds that can mistake truths.

Abundant conference. This course Moses prescribed to the Israelites to remember the laws given unto them, that they should often talk of them to their children. Conference is as the driving in of the nail; one remembers that which the other forgets. Our memories help our lips, and our lips strengthen our memories.

Diligent practice. The scholar, by daily writing the copy, thereby mends his hand and helps his memory. Truths are ordained for practice. It cannot be but that truths should remain faithful in the memory which are made faithful in our walking. Truths easily take their leave of those who oppose them or do not act them.

Chapter 4

The Second Proposition

PROPOSITION 2. Acceptance of truths is not sufficient, but there must be persistence in them ("and hold fast").

Saint Paul is much in this doctrine: "Hold fast the form of sound words," 2 Timothy 1:13. So again in Titus 1:9, "Hold fast the faithful word." And that this doctrine may not be thought proper and peculiar to the preacher of the truth, but common to all Christians, he therefore enlarges the precept to all the Romans (and under them to all Christians) to adhere or cleave unto what is good. The word in the original is that they should be glued unto it. Solomon in effect delivers the same in Proverbs 23:23: "Buy the truth and sell it not." A man may lawfully sell his house and lands as the apostles did, and follow Christ, and in some sense his wife and children (as Jerome in *Epist. ad Heliod* would rather than he would put off Christ), yes, and his own life too, as Saint Paul did, and not count it dear for Christ. But the truth must not be sold. It must be kept as a thing exceeding all price and bargain.

Now for the fuller understanding of this proposition, premise with me these particulars:

1. I speak not of human and moral truths, such as are the rules in secular arts in which there may be, and is, many times, an infallibility, but of reli-

77

gious and divine truths which are contained in the Word of God.

2. Religious truths are so either in the imagination of man or in the reality of the thing. I am not bound to embrace, much less to persist in, all which every man propounds for truths, or which he conjectures to be so. Only I am to hold fast those truths which the Word (rightly and genuinely expounded) teaches and determines to be so.

3. Again, the truths which seem to own themselves on the Word of God are either immediate and expressed, or only mediate and deduced. Expressed truths are to be held fast, but deduced truths which are then collected by the medium of a man's ability to judge, are to be tried and examined by the prime and immediate truths, and are so far to be held as they are found (upon due search) to have conformity with the immediate and express rules of truth.

4. Expressed truths (suppose them to be known and received) may be considered either in the latitude of them or with restriction. We may not think it sufficient to hold fast some particular truths, either the greater or the lesser, and leave the rest to shift for themselves. But all known truths, even those which are not of that main concern, not any one of them must be forsaken or left, but retained and maintained as Athanasius and others of the first Nicene Fathers would not diminish, or add one iota and title about the deity of Christ. Or as Moses would not leave one hoof behind, so we must not renounce or forsake any one branch of known truth, seem it never so little in the eyes of men.

5. Though there is a difference of times, yet there

ought to be no difference of holy truths. There are times of prosperity for the gospel, as Constantine's time was to the church, and there are times of calamity, as Nero's time, and Dioclesian's, and others of the persecuting emperors.

Truth must be held fast, yes, all truth, at all times; you see that the stars shine in the coldest night of winter, as well as in the calmest night of summer. So truths must be held in the worst as well as in the best days.

Josephus reports of the Samaritans that if any good and favor befell the Jews, then they would pretend affinity and kindred with them, they came from Jacob; but if any calamity, then they were none of the stock of Abraham. It must not be thus with us to vary our hearty respect to truths according to the favor or discouragement that the world bestows upon them. But to cleave unto them as Saint Paul did, under the sword, as St. Ignatius among the wild beasts, and Laurentius on the gridiron, and Daniel among the lions, and the three children in the fiery furnace.

6. Though there is a difference of persons, yet we must not differ and wave our respects to holy truths. Perhaps those holy truths which you have heard and tried and received may be contradicted and disputed, by some bold schismatic, heretical brains, who would blur and dim the truth so that they may bring in damnable doctrines. By these they may be disgraced, derided, and reproached; these dogs may bark against the moon and its light. Yes, or perhaps though they have forwardly courted and professed the truths, yet they may fall off with

Hymenaeus and Philetus, and turn into vile apostates.

But as Peter said of Christ, that you must say and act of truths: "Though all men should forsake you, yet I will never forsake you." Against all subtlety of disputes, variety of judgments, schism and malice of evil men, and inconstancy of some men, you must be rightly balanced. "Hold fast the truth which thou hast heard and received."

QUESTION. But how must truths be held fast?

ANSWER. In four respects:

1. In the judgment and understanding.
2. In the will and affection.
3. In profession.
4. In conversation and practice.

1. In the judgment and understanding, for assent and approbation, there must be a firm evidence of them. I confess that there is a latitude in our credence, upon more and more evidence of truth, there may be a further and stronger assent unto them, and approbation of them. But there must be no wavering in the judgment; we must not admit of a staggering and reeling mind, nor of a levity in our judgments, to be driven and carried about with every wind of doctrine, as the Apostle speaks in Ephesians 4:14. Athanasius knew this well when he held his judgment fast in the truth of the deity of Christ against the Arians. So Saint Augustine held his judgment fast in the doctrine of grace against the Pelagians, and Cyprian against the Donatists, or Novatians, or Catharists.

It is an honor for a man to recant an error, but a

treacherous shame for any Christian to suffer any truth to be supplanted by any error.

2. In the will and affection. Our love must hold the truth fast, therefore the Apostle bids us to be glued unto it, Romans 12:9. It is with truths as with some plants which live and thrive not except in warm climates.

That ancient desire after truth and delight in it, to take counsel from it, and strength from it, and comfort by it, must not decay and die within us, but must remain and abound. Though others hate, disgrace, and endeavor to make void the truth, yet we must cleave unto it, and love it, as David did in Psalm 119.

3. In our profession. Hence that advice of the Apostle in Philippians 2:15 to "hold forth the Word of Life, even in the midst of a dark and forward generation." Christ would have us not only to believe, but confess Him before men. Remember that it was no small sin in Peter when he pretended that he knew not the man. Gregory Nazianzen reports, in one of his orations against Julian, that some Christian soldiers, being cunningly circumvented by him to idolatrous sacrifices and perceiving the error, all ran back unto him and threw him his money again, and protested they were Christians, and in what they did, they were circumvented by him, Hebrews 10:23: "Let us hold fast the profession of our faith without wavering." The Christian must neither change his Master, nor his service, nor his livery.

4. In our conversation. We must still practice truths and keep our lives answerable unto them.

Saint John calls this walking in the truth. Then a man walks in the truth when he holds on his course of holy obedience to it against all the encouragements and discouragements of the world, as the three children in Daniel. Not with the Galatians, beginning in the Spirit and ending in the flesh, or like those Israelites whose righteousness was as the morning dew, but we must still run the race set before us, and keep steadfast our feet unto the paths of righteousness and ways of truth.

QUESTION. Why must divine truths heard and received be held fast?

ANSWER. Reasons thereof are many. I will briefly point out some of them:

1. Divine truth is a most precious and excellent thing; therefore in Scripture it is compared to gold, which of metals is the most precious. Nay, it is more precious than gold or rubies, and all the things which you can desire are not to be compared unto it (see Proverbs 3:14-15). It is more excellent than the excellencies of the creatures—not than some of them, but than all of them. And if a man were to imagine any excellency, or if the utmost of his desires were enlarged, yet could they not find out and pitch upon such an excellency. Therefore said Saint John to the church of Philadelphia, in Revelation 3:11: "Hold that fast which thou hast, that no man take thy crown." The crown is the top of royalties; such a thing is truth, so let no man take your crown.

Beloved, there are two properties which assure us of the excellency of things:

First, the more holy they are, the more excellent

they are. All corruptions are diminutions of excellency: the more mixed a thing is, the more it is abased—as if gold and tin be mixed—and the more pure it is, as mere gold, the more glorious it is. Now the truths of God are holy, not as persons are holy (which is with mixture and imperfection), but as the light at noon day is pure without darkness at all.

Second, the more that God is in anything, the more excellent it is, for so much as we partake of Him (who is excellency itself), so much more we rise in our excellence.

But the great God is altogether seen in this Word of Truth. There is His wisdom; there is His power and greatness; there is His love and mercifulness; there is His Christ and faithfulness. Therefore it is most excellent and, consequently, to be held fast by us.

2. Divine truths are (as it were) made over to us under terms of constancy and perpetuity. I find in Scriptures that they are termed sometimes.

Our heritage states, which are personal (if that is the phrase), for possession may be sold, as that which a child buys with his own money; but states which are natural or hereditary, such I mean as come to be ours by descent, ought to be kept for posterity. "God forbid," said Naboth, "that I should sell the inheritance of my fathers." Divine truths are a heritage to descend from us to our children, and therefore we are neither to dispossess ourselves of them nor to suffer ourselves by any to be dispossessed of them. Psalm 119:111: "Thy testimonies have I taken as an heritage forever."

God's trust is either something we commit to

God or something God commits to us. 2 Timothy 1:12: "He is able to keep that which I have committed unto Him." We trust God with our souls, and God trusts us with His truths, which are therefore called "that good thing committed to us for to keep" in 2 Timothy 1:14. Now in matters of trust we must be faithful, or we must be responsible for the whole wherewith we are instructed, as the servants in the gospel, who had talents committed to their trust, were called to account for them. So if the Lord trusts any man with graces, or with His truths, the man must carefully keep and preserve them, for the Lord will ask him another day for His trust, as Saint John did of the bishop of Jerusalem for his deposit.

They observe that a trust must be, first, redelivered, second, wholly, third, only to him who committed it to us for trust.

3. Not to hold fast the truths is an exceeding and fearful injury or wrong. It is injurious:

To God, for He is the Lord or God of Truth. Truths are ours for the efficacy of them, but only His for the authority of them. A private person must not presume of himself to sell the king's jewels. He reveals them. He owns them. He has sealed them with the blood of Christ. And, therefore, you presumptuously wrong the Lord to put off the things which belong to Him.

To our covenant and vow. What was our baptism but a devoting and solemn vowing of ourselves to be faithful to Christ and His truths? We solemnly professed that none should be our Lord but God, and that we would be His faithful servants unto our lives' end. Yes, and we have ratified this vow many a time by coming to the Sacrament of the Lord's Supper.

Now if we do not hold fast the truths of Christ, but forsake all of them or any of them, we are guilty of extreme perjury—not in a matter between man and man, but between God and man. You are sworn again and again unto the Lord your God, and have (as much as in you lies) made void the covenant of grace and life for your poor soul.

4. Consider the necessary uses of divine truths, and then we will acknowledge that they are to be held fast.

The use of the Word or divine truths respects the everlasting and happy condition of the soul from the beginning to the end thereof. Everlasting and true happiness is the end and scope that every Christian looks at; and divine truths serve him fully and effectually to this end: both to discover it and to bring man unto it.

There are many things required to set us in the true way, to bring a man to heaven:

Conviction of his sinful condition. But the Word enlightens the mind and convinces the conscience.

Contrition for sin. But the Word pricks our hearts, as Acts 2, and humbles them.

Conversion of soul. But the Law of the Lord is perfect, converting the soul, Psalm 19:7. By it comes faith into the soul, which gets Christ, Romans 10:17, and by it comes repentance, Acts 3:19.

Augmentation of grace. But by the Word we are built up, Acts 20:32, and grow more and more.

Perseverance in grace. But by the Word we are kept and established to the end; it is the power of God unto salvation, Romans 1:16.

What should I say more? Read the Apostle summing up all in *2* Timothy 3:16–17: "All Scripture is given by inspiration of God, and is profitable for doctrine, for reproof, for correction, for instruction in righteousness: that the man of God may be perfect, thoroughly furnished to all good works."

And verse 15: "Yes, they are able to make us wise unto salvation, through faith which is in Christ Jesus."

Again, there are many comforting and supporting encouragements in our ways as divine consolations of the Spirit of God—peace in conscience, joy in the Holy Ghost—all which are the myrrh dropping only from divine truths. "Thy Word has comforted me," said David. "Thy Word has quickened me." In the house of his pilgrimage they were the joys of his heart, and in the days of his calamity they were the stay of his heart.

Now put all together: if divine truths show us true happiness, if they only put us unto the true way, unto that true happiness, if they only keep us in that way, if they only comfort and strengthen us in that way, if they only bring us to the end of our faith, even the salvation of our souls, will we not, ought we not to hold them fast?

The first use of this point shall be to convince and reprove the wonderful inconstancy of the sons of men, that slipperiness and unsettledness of spirit which is to be found among them.

Consider divine truths as they lay:

1. In doctrine. We may now complain as the Apostle did of the Galatians, chapter 1:6: "I marvel that ye are so soon removed from him that called

you into the grace of Christ, unto another gospel."

Some revolt from the Protestant doctrine to the popish leven; others fall off from the orthodox articles of our church to Anabaptist fancies and Socinian blasphemies; and the Lord is merciful unto us. What daily unsettledness and giddiness possesses us? If any novelty of doctrine (though a root of bitterness) starts up and is delivered with any confidence or cunning or deceiving wit, how instantly we fly off from our old truths, how greedily and madly we suck in poison errors! And being thus driven with every wind, what tempests of railing and disgraces do we heap upon those who cross our fickleness with constant vindications and assertings of the true doctrines of faith and life!

It makes me to pity this great and famous city, while I behold a very rabble of all opinions, and such a going and coming, touchings at and fallings off from the land of uprightness. One week this is a truth, and almost an article; the next week it is no such matter, but some other thing is the right.

Thus we play many times with great truths as children do with their dolls: while one embraces them, another breaks and throws them into the dirt.

But are there so many ways to heaven as men will make, or have you power to coin other articles of faith at pleasure, or will the Lord bear all this resting and mocking with His truths? Two things make me fear the Lord will punish us in the gospel—our general barrenness in life and our great fickleness in matter of truths.

2. In conversation. Many times we hold the truth in unrighteousness. We do not prize the truth

and love it, nor live according to it with constancy, but as the prophet cried out, "How is the beautiful city become an heap?" So may we say of many, "How is their righteous walking degenerated into an ungodly living?" Their wine is soured and lamp put out.

But I will tell you the reasons and causes of all this inconstancy and apostasy:

REASON 1. Men are very ignorant and, therefore, very inconstant. Ignorance is the great sponge to suck in errors, as pride is the great bawd to vent them. Chastity may be tossed any way; that which is weak is also light.

REASON 2. Though their apprehensions are large, yet their affections are foul; they know truth, but love sin which is contrary to truth. Now a foul stomach ever makes an ill head, and a secret love of sin works out the strength of truth in the mind. Men more easily grow erroneous who first grow irreligious.

REASON 3. There is an itch of pride. Eve and Adam wanted to know more than was fit, and therefore lost all that was good. You never read of a proud person but either his life was notoriously tainted or his judgment notably corrupted. The greatest errors have fallen from those who have been most proud, and have been taken up by those who have been most ignorant.

REASON 4. And then also many have Athenian wits: they long for novelties, though the old wine is best; yet their palate must be in the fashion for new. There is a sore vanity in a natural mind that it cannot long fix on any state or on any truth.

REASON 5. A deceitful slavishness. Many give up their souls and faith to the religion of others, and like wax, are still fashioned to the opinions of great persons. They are afraid of their displeasures, and therefore, even in points of religion, will dance after their pipe.

REASON 6. A sordid and eminent love of the world, for which Demas forsook Christ, Judas sold his Master, and Hymeneus made shipwreck of faith. The unsatisfiable slave to the world will never be a faithful servant to truth. He who has already pawned his soul will, with as much ease, sell off the truth. Spira, for its sake, abjured the truth, but ventured the loss of it, and himself too.

REASON 7. Many men are licentious and, therefore, unsteadfast. Corrupt doctrines give more scope than the true and heavenly. We are apt to believe that sooner which pleases us most. Erroneous points are more for pleasure, and divine truths are more for strictness, and therefore, as those Grecians (if I forget not the story) gave up their weapons to enjoy the sports, so many give up the truth to enjoy their easy and loose kind of walk.

But for you, I hope better things, though I thus speak: hitherto you have heard the good truths and ways of God, and have held them fast. I have not found you (as other people) of so unsettled and inconstant spirits. And therefore, as Christ said to the church of Thyatira, the same I will presume to say unto you, Revelation 2:24–25, I will put upon you no other burden but that which ye have already, "hold fast." Why do I need to urge this with many motives?

If it is truth, why should it be left? Is error better

than truth? Then should darkness be better than light?

Can you better your states by leaving of truth? When the devils fell from truth, they fell from heaven. When Adam fell from the truth, he fell from paradise.

Will not the truth keep you? If you keep the truth as the ship does the pilot who keeps it, truth will keep your soul and graces together, your soul and Christ together, your soul and comfort together, your soul and prosperity together; therefore it is called the girdle of truth because, as a girdle, it holds all together. You part with strength, with joy, with safety, with blessing, with happiness if you part with truth.

The reward is sure if you are faithful—not a mean reward, but that of life, even a crown of life, Revelation 2:10.

Now that you may forever hold fast divine truths, take these rules or directions:

RULE 1. Lay a solid foundation in distinct knowledge of them; confused brains cause unsettled hearts. Rest not in Pilate's demand of "what is truth?", nor in the Israelites hovering between two opinions, nor in that gross mockery of religion, to take up truth upon trust for any man's sake whatsoever. Were he the sharpest Jeremiah, or the most learned Paul, or the most comfortable Barnabas, be not satisfied this is truth because this man said it, but as the honorable Bereans searched the Scriptures about the things which even Saint Paul himself delivered, so do you. "Prove all things," said the

Apostle. Receive truth upon an evidence of truth; if the first truth (which is the Word of God) and the rule and compass will not approve it, it is error and not truth.

QUESTION. Yes, but how may we know truths? For there are many religions, and many opinions obtruded to the world, the truth of which cannot so easily be discerned.

I answer that true doctrine may be discerned from false doctrines:

By the unity of them. Truth is one or not. There is but one way (said Aristotle) to hit the mark, but many ways to miss it. Error is manifold and divers, like the image which Nebuchadnezzar saw mixed of gold and clay. Aristotle speaks of vices, that they are contrary both to virtues and themselves. So erroneous doctrines are opposed to truth and themselves. There is no error but is like a liar, apt to forget the wound itself; but truth is single, like Christ's garment, undivided. As there is but one Christ, so there is but one faith.

The purity of them. All false doctrine (like treacherous medicine) gives ease; or like a whore who is much in beauty when false in honesty. What it wants in verity, it makes up in liberty; like ill wares which therefore have the larger allowances. The doctrine which is unsound generally is licentious, as is evident in the Mohammedan or popish tenants.

But truth is holy in itself, and to us, teaching it within the heart, and ordering it in the life. It is an adversary to sin because all sin is an adversary unto God.

The efficacy of them. Usually corrupt doctrines add

to our notions, but meddle not with our corruptions. They swell us, but do not edify us; they are pills which only work upon the brain; they neither bring true grace or sound peace with them. Only this, Satan makes the erroneous very violent that thereby they may think themselves in the right.

But the doctrine which is true is strong; it is heavenly in its nature and mighty in its operation. It comes *from* God and brings *to* God; it makes the bad good and the good better. There is no such salve to heal a corrupt heart, nor balm to refresh a troubled conscience, like truth.

The antiquity of them. Error is but the shadow and ape of truth. Truth is the first born, for God spoke it, before the devil spoke the other. Errors may be old, but truth saw the light before them, the whole hodgepodge of corrupt doctrines among the papists, such as transubstantiation, the invocation of saints, prayers for the dead, merit, and supremacy—their origins were from yesterday. Though they boast antiquity, yet they dare not stand to the trial of Christ and His apostles, who must decide all truths.

The simplicity of them. Errors came in by the serpent at the first, and constitute much of its nature; it is full of windings and turnings. All corrupt doctrines are deceivable and subtle. How many arts were feigned by Arius and the Arian bishops, to bring in their damnable error? What forging of lies and odious accusations of Athansius, that he was dishonest with a woman and cut off a man's hand, as Eusebius relates. And so the Jesuites about Calvin and Luther, and Melancthon and Beza. For the establishing of the Council of Trent, the Pope's cloak bags were weekly filled with devices and carriages.

Yes, and observe the very Papists at this day, how deceivably confident they are that all antiquity and testimony is on their side, when either it is a pack of their own writers only, or other authors which they have forged, or else antiquity miserably lanced and cut and interlaced by their *Index expurgatorius.* Yes, and I pray God that many of the opinions in this city are not bolstered up with high clamors and artificial lies. But truth is naked and plain: it is neither of a cruel nature, like Cain, nor of a subtle spirit with Absolom, nor of a lying spirit with Ahab's false prophets; it flatters no man, nor beguiles any. Being truth, it is not ashamed of light or trial; and it alone can maintain itself against all contrary quarrels. A good cause is like a good conscience, even a bulwark to itself, like the sun in its light and heat against all clouds.

The duration of them. Truth, like the sun, has run down through all ages. Not that all men have embraced it, but that by some it has still been embraced. Some one or more have still been at the bar to bear witness unto it. New men have still risen up (and sometimes out of the ashes, as it were, of the dead) to maintain, and either by tongue or pen or blood to defend the truth.

But erroneous doctrines, as they want an inward harmony, so also an outward consent. Like a deceitful brook, they are spent after awhile, or like commotions in a state, though strong or long, yet they come to an end at length. Either some special judgments on the ringleaders, or the authority of princes, as Alexander against Arius, or the prayers of the saints, or the decision of lawful counsels have still cashiered these meteors. But as it is said of divine mercy, that it endures forever, the same is affirmed of divine truth; it runs from one generation to another. Till Christ makes His church triumphant, the militant church shall be the pillar of truth.

The conformity of them to rule or word. Erroneous doctrines, like unsound flesh, cannot abide handling, and like an ill-favored woman, would have all looking-glasses broken.

But truth, like sound gold, will endure a touchstone. Truth will be found truth upon search; bring it to the conscience, it will work as truth. Bring it to the death bed; it will uphold as truth; bring it to the Scriptures, it will hold out as truth.

When truths upon search are found to be truths, then embrace them for the truth's sake, not upon personal and mutable causes or ends.

Firm resolutions after trial, by which our knowledge comes to the clear; and without doubt there must be now a plain resolution and purpose of heart in cleaving to such faithfully evidenced truths. You must, by an immovable faith (as it were) root your every heart in the truths of Christ, as was the case with Saint Paul: through bonds and afflictions, through good report or evil, through death itself abides for Christ, "Come what will come, disputes, fancies, errors, troubles, losses, I have found the truth, and it will I hold forever."

Loyal affection is loyal when it is inclusive to every truth, and exclusive to nothing but truth. This loyal affection will make us to, first, do, second, suffer, and third, cleave. Love truth, and then truth will be held. "I held him and would not let him go," said the church, then in love with Christ, Song of Solomon 3. Love is the easiest key to open the heart to Christ, and the strongest lock to keep sure the truth in our hearts. When you have experimentally felt the heavenly strength and comfort of God's truths, then will you certainly stick unto them.

Join conscience to science. O when people have the truths still sounding in their ears, and ungodliness still stirring and ruling in their lives, it cannot be that they should have strong hands who have wicked hearts. Hymeneus made shipwreck both of faith and conscience together, 1 Timothy 1:19.

Therefore strive to obey the truths: add to your faith virtue; be a doing Christian as well as a knowing Christian.

Be watchful in prayer to God, with David, to uphold you; with Saint Peter to establish you, still to keep you, that you may keep his truths. Excellent is that speech that God by whose light alone we know the truth, by His strength alone we keep it.

Thus much for the text, and now for the occasion; and here I cannot be long. Neither my affections nor yours will admit of large discourse, only a word *of* you and a word *to* you.

Of you, so regardful have you been to my ministry, so loving to my person, so faithful in your maintenance, so cheerfully encouraging, generally from you all, but chiefly from the chiefest, that had it pleased the Lord to have given me health (the which I have scarce enjoyed one whole year together since I have been here), I should not have stirred easily from such a people for the best preferment that could be conveniently offered unto me.

I speak my heart freely. I cannot tell on which side the unwillingness is most, whether on your part who are left or on my part who am constrained to leave you.

But to say no more of your goodness, give me leave (for the close of all) to leave a few legacies with you, being all my friends, and hearken to my words, as the words of a dying man, for the Lord knows how short my days may be.

My legacies are these:

1. Lay out more time for your souls. The soul is a precious thing; the soul is a corrupted thing; sins are in it; much guilt is upon it; there is a Christ that it needs, holiness that it must have, heaven that it would have. Your body is but clay, your soul a spirit, the world a vanity, your soul immortal. All is well if the soul is well; nothing is well if that is evil. I beseech you to pray more, hear more, know more, confer more, do more and more for your souls; and when you come to die you will then find it to be all your work. O then while health is in you, make it your kingdom of heaven and the righteousness thereof for your souls; feed not the slave and starve the child.

2. Upon good grounds make sure of a reconciled God; live not in an unreconciled condition. There are no enemies like an ill conscience and a good God. Study the sight of your sins and the blood of Christ, repentance from dead works and faith in

the Lord Jesus; so shall you behold the face of God and live. The ways of reconciliation with God and the settling of your conscience about it may cost you many prayers and tears and diligent studies, but the love of God and heaven will answer and recompense all.

3. Wisely improve all heavenly seasons. The Lord hitherto has continued unto you days of peace and salvation, heavenly opportunities public and private, and I beseech Him forever so to do. Now receive not the grace of God in vain; lay hold on these occasions. If there is no wisdom to improve them, there may be sadness for neglecting them. You see how many worthy and faithful ministers God has taken away (of late) by death, and shall the present prophets live forever? O then, in your day and time hearken, regard, repent, believe, live, and thrive under holy and faithful ministers. Make more use of their doctrines, of their rules, of their counsels, of their comforts, and of their experience and prayers. The night will come when neither we nor you must work any longer.

4. Study the grounds and principles of religion better. First, lay good foundations and then build on them. Errors in the entrance weaken all in the progress. Take pains to know what that good and acceptable will of the Lord is. A well-bottomed Christian is like a well-bottomed vessel at sea which can ride out in all weathers. No Christian stands so fast, or thrives so well, as the well-grounded Christian.

5. Be rather an agent than a disputant in religion. The vanity of wit is to argue much, but the sin-

cerity of the heart is to do much. For doubtful points and subtle novelties, let others beat and serve them; and, in the meanwhile, pray much that you may obey the truths you know. In speculative things, be wise to sobriety; in practical things, be as good as you can. It is not the wittiest scholar, but the truest Christian who shall go to heaven.

6. Be less formal and more fruitful. Know that as we must be brought to an account for every word which we speak, so much more for every word that God speaks.

Mere godliness is not enough under constant and great means of grace. God expects much when He gives much. If it does not utterly cast you, yet it must excessively trouble you to be thin in bearing when God has been large in sowing.

7. Let all Christians be of more fruitful hearts and charitable spirits one towards another. There are treacherous and malicious hearts enough in the world; you need not to help the devil to be an accuser of the brethren. It is a sad thing when one Christian can hardly trust another, and that they who should pity and heal infirmities are yet inventors of lies and reproaches. "These are the wounds which my friends gave me," said the Church in Song of Solomon. If your fellow Christian fails, be compassionate and succor him rather than hate and reproach him. You shall never establish your graces or name upon the ruins and scandals of another man. If you are a strong Christian, be more tender; if weak, be more silent. The strong should bear the infirmities of the weak, and the weak should hearken to the directions of the strong, and safety surer by

love than by division. Therefore be of one mind and live in peace; let brotherly love continue.

8. Mind death often, and prepare for it betimes. He who is a stranger to dying thoughts is ordinarily a stranger to a godly life. You would hasten and better your work if you look back more on your life and more forward on your death.

9. Be diligent in your particular places. The idle body can hardly hold a good soul. That man is in danger who is all for heaven or all for earth; both our callings must be regarded.

10. Be much in prayer. The Christian usually gets the greatest blessings on his knees. God is much with him in grace who is most with God in prayer.

And pray not for yourselves only, but for others. And as for others, so for me, as Saint Paul desired of the Ephesians in 6:19–20: "that utterance may be given unto me, that I may open my mouth boldly to make known the mystery of the gospel, that therein I may speak as I ought to speak." And so as the same Apostle said to those Ephesians, the same I say unto you.

Brethren, I commend you unto God, and to the Word of His grace, which is able to build up, and to give you an inheritance among all them which are sanctified.

Finis

"England's Preservation"

"Thus saith the Lord to the men of Judah and Jerusalem, 'Break up your fallow ground, and sow not among thorns'." Jeremiah 4:3

PART ONE
"Break up your fallow ground."

There is a learned writer (Bernard) who speaks of four days for a sinner.

The first is a day of loathsomeness, and this is the time when the sinner lies rotting in the grave of sin.

The second is a day of anguish, and this is the time when conscience begins to be awakened with the sight and sense of sin.

The third day is a day of mourning, and this is the time when the heart begins to melt into tears for sinning.

The fourth is a day of combat, and this is the time when the penitent and converted soul sets itself against the temptation of sin.

The first of these is the worst of our days, and yet too common (the dead in this sense are more than the living). The second of these is a bitter and turbulent day, and yet it may prove happy and cheerful (there being more hope of a sore conscience than of a seared conscience). The last two are, like pre-

101

cious jewels, very good, but very rare. It is an easy thing to find sinners, but it is not an easy thing to find mourning sinners and penitent sinners.

So blind is the mind of man, so perverse is the will of a sinner, so prevalent is the love of sin, so desperate is the resolution of a hardened heart that neither the golden scepter nor the iron rod, neither the sweetest mercies nor the sharpest miseries will easily prevail with a sinning man to become a penitent man. But though God is leaving, though mercies are setting, though wrath is approaching, though life is short, though hell is fearful, yet it is a thousand to one that the sinner remains constantly wicked or only deceitfully good.

You have a clear instance in the Jews in this chapter, who, notwithstanding that they had almost sinned away their God, their country, their lives, their helps, and their hopes, and notwithstanding all their warnings by a variety of prophets, and all their sufferings by a variety of punishments, and all their threatenings by a variety of judgments, though there was but a step between them and death, only one mercy between them and utter destruction by the enemy, yet either they totally neglected the work, or would not be persuaded thoroughly to act the duty of repentance.

The Lord saw this dangerous obstinace and pitied it. He strove with them to save their souls that they might, by this means, save their country. The way He spread before them is expressed partly in verse 1: " 'If thou wilt return, O Israel!' saith the Lord, 'return unto Me, and if thou wilt put away thine abominations out of My sight, then thou shalt not remove'.'" Leave your sins and save all. You have made many overtures and semblances thereof by fastings, by confessings, and by prayings. Now I add one thing more. Repent in good earnest. This will be life to your solemnities and safety to your nation.

The way is also expressed partly in verse 3: "Break up your fallow ground and sow not among thorns." If you do not repent, you are undone; if you do repent, but not thoroughly, you will be undone too. Hypocrisy in good duties as well as profaneness in bad ways may ruin a person and nation. A man may be as surely drowned in a ship that has a leak as when he has no ship at all.

Therefore, pretend repentance no longer, but act it; and when you act it, do not act it slightly, but exactly. Become good, and do good to purpose. If you regard and follow this counsel, then, as in verse 1, you shall not remove. But if you will not hearken to it, then, as in verse 4, "My fury shall come forth forth like fire, and burn so that none can quench it because of the evil of your doings."

The words of my text contain in them the principal works of this day, which are two:

1. A serious humiliation, unto which the Jews are exhorted in these words: "Break up your fallow ground."

2. A dextrous reformation, delivered unto them by way of caution: "And sow not among thorns."

There must not be a little raising, but a breaking, and not a mere breaking, but a breaking up; and when that is done there must be a sowing too, but every sowing must not serve the turn. It must be such a sowing as may come to something. It must not be a sowing among thorns.

The field which I am at this time to work upon and go over is very large. There is much more ground in it than I can conveniently break up and sow. I shall, though, by that God's assistance who alone is the Maker and Breaker of hearts, set upon the whole work, and hope that He, in tender mercy, may so accompany and water and prosper His truths this day that all our fallow grounds may be broken up, and then so graciously sow in righteousness that we and all the land may shortly reap in mercy!

I begin with the first part: "Break up your fallow ground."

These words are to be understood not literally, but metaphorically. I make no question that any who hears me *does* question. Interpreters, though, vary sometimes in their conjectures. Tertullian, by fallow ground, understands the old Law, which he says is to be broken up by the new Law (he means the gospel), an exposition greatly impertinent and too wide. Cassianus understands it to be the heathens, the pagans and other secular persons; nor is this conjecture apt to the text.

Cyprian draws nearest to the sense who, by fallow ground, understands the conversations of the Jews. Cyril of Alexander thinks it is a heart like the wilderness, wild and destitute of all pious culture. And Chrysostom understands more exactly, by fallow ground, the very core and depths of a sinful heart.

So then, to stop all quotations, the fallow ground is nothing else but the sinful estate of a person or nation. And it is very aptly so described by reason of that consimiltude which the one has with the other.

For, first, fallow ground is a barren piece of earth, void of all excellency and beauty. There is not one grain of good seed in it, nor any one delightful flower. Such a desert is man's sinful heart. It is very vanity and vanity, no divine excellency to be found there. Not any one effect, nor any one seed of spiritual inclination. For this, it may answer as the depth did for wisdom, "It is not in me," Job 28:14.

Second, fallow ground is usually an indigested thicket, lumbered all over with weeds, briars, thorns, and thistles (that original curse which befell the earth for man's transgression). And such a piece also is man's sinful heart. Though it is but a barren wilderness for any good, yet it is an ample ocean for all that is evil and hurtful. The upper part of his field has in it an abundance of thorns (unprofitable thoughts, hurtful cares, wounding errors), and the lower part of his field is as full of stinking weeds (vile affections, as the Apostle calls them). The best fruits of him are but as a briar to scratch himself, and to catch and entangle others with sin.

Lastly, fallow ground is a hardened part of earth, extremely compacted by the influences of the sun and winds, and by its own native inclination. So it is not an easy thing to sever and dispose it for a better use. Just so is a natural or sinful heart. It is so trodden and feared and obdurated, partly by the frequent repetition of sinful acts and partly by the intention of sinful delights, that it is not only defective of good, but also very active against it—unyielding, resisting, and fighting against all heavenly counsels and motions. The man is evil, and will be so. He is not good, nor will he be so, unless God, by an insuperable virtue of His own Spirit makes him to be so.

We have found what the fallow ground is. Let us in the next place inquire what the breaking up of it is. The fallow ground is broken up when the husbandman comes with his plow and enters that plow into it. He deeply enters it, even to the bowels of the ground, and then rents and tears and turns it upside down. And not in just one furrow, but in every furrow: once, twice, perhaps thrice if need so requires.

Even so the sinful heart is broken up when the Almighty and gracious God (whom Christ calls the husbandman) comes with His Word and Spirit, and enters into the heart or soul of a sinner by irresistible convincings, and by efficacious humblings (which are as rentings and tearings to the ground), and by rooting up the dominion and love of all sins.

The Scriptures sometimes call this work a touching, sometimes a pricking, sometimes a troubling, sometimes a wounding, sometimes a bruising, sometimes a breaking, sometimes a renting, sometimes a killing, and sometimes a humbling and melting of the heart.

And this is that which God calls for in the text from the Jews as a means to prevent their utter destruction by the sword of the Caldeans, whence the proposition which I shall in the first place insist on is this:

DOCTRINE 1. The breaking up of sinful hearts is a singular means to prevent the breaking down of a sinful nation.

There are three things which I shall speak to for the explication of this assertion:

1. What the right breaking of a sinful heart is

which is so available to prevent the breaking down of a sinful nation.

2. Some demonstrations that it is a preventing means.

3. The reasons why it is so.

QUESTION 1. What is the right breaking of a sinful heart?

ANSWER. Be pleased to know there is a twofold breaking of a sinful heart.

1. One is specious only and formal, as artificial jugglers seem to wound themselves, but do not; or as players seem to thrust themselves through their bodies, but the sword only passes through their clothes. There is something done *about* sins, but nothing is done *against* sins. Sins are hurt, but not removed, as the same author speaks, which he truly calls a fiction and vanity. When men only lop the trees, in time they grow faster and thicker. Against this breaking the prophet of old complained greatly. In Isaiah, they hung down their heads and afflicted their souls for a day, but for all that they still afflicted their poor brethren. And in Hosea they howled, but yet they still rebelled against the Lord. In Malachi they cried out and covered the altar with tears, and yet, for all their pretended condition, they profaned the holiness of God. And though the Pharisees assumed unto themselvs a most mortified garb of humbling, especially in their days of fasting, disfiguring their faces as Christ reported, yet their hearts were as loose, as full of pride, covetousness, envy, and opposition of Christ as ever.

2. Another is serious and real, which is acted

most in the hidden man and pierces like the Word
(Hebrews 4:12), even to the dividing of soul and
spirit, of which likewise there are two kinds. One is
called attrition, and the other is called contrition by
the Schoolmen. The former, by our casuists, is
called a legal breaking, and the latter an evangelical
breaking.

They distinguish them partly:

By their objects. Penal evil is the object on which attrition works; and sinful evil is the object on which
contrition works. The one is conversant about passive evil, that is, the evil which we suffer; the other is
conversant about active evil, that is, the evil which
we have done. For sin has in it two qualities: one to
make us unhappy (and at this attrition looks), another to make us unholy (and at this contrition
looks).

By their causes. Legal attrition is only the pinching
of servile fear and despair, for it sees nothing but
what will tear and distract the conscience. But
evangelical contrition is the melting and lamenting
of filial love and hope. The frowns of a revenging
judge cause that, but the smiles of a gracious father
raise this. In the one the heart is shivered by the
flashes of hell; in the other the heart is melted by
the beams of heaven. A stroke from guilt broke
Judas's heart into despair, but a look from Christ
broke Peter's heart into tears.

By their effects. An attrite heart may (for that space
of time while the conscience burns and flames with
wrath) become negatively penitent. It does not purpose to sin. The sensible anguish for former sinnings may suspend delightful intentions for future

sins, but the contrite heart (out of a contrariety of nature) becomes positively holy. It cordially purposes not to sin any more. All which, if I mistake not, is the same that Cajetan means when he says that attrition produces an imperfect motion, but contrition produces a complete and direct will against sin.

But this discourse, I fear, is too speculative for this day's work. Give me leave, therefore, to open the nature of this penitential heart breaking in a more practical and profitable way. There are several workings which ordinarily concur to the full constituting of this heart-breaking work, whereof some are antecedent, some are formally ingredient, and some are inseparably consequent.

Antecedent Workings

The antecedent workings are such as previously led the way to the evangelical breaking as the needle does to the thread and the hammer's breaking does to the melting by the fire, by way of order only and not by causality. These are principally three:

First, a notional irradiation. The Lord never breaks a sinner's heart before He has opened a sinner's eyes. The day breaks before the heart breaks. Light breaks to elevate the soul thus far to discern and distinguish evil. Till then, sin is no burden to the conscience, nor trouble to the affections. As no good wrapped up in darkness excites desire, so no evil swathed up in ignorance strikes any trouble or sorrow. Unknown things have no motive faculty because they are as nothing at all. And therefore God

ever keeps this method to make sin appear to be sin
and afterwards to humble and break our hearts for
it.

Second, a practical conviction, which is nothing
else but a personal application of guilt and wrath,
without which the notion of sin would be no trouble. Let me open my mind unto you: drunkenness,
swearing, whoredom, murder, and Sabbath-breaking
are sins. And such persons who are guilty of them,
without repentance, "shall not inherit the kingdom
of God." All this the sinner knows already, and yet is
not troubled; for as long as light rests in a bare notion it is only an addition to his understanding. It is
no burden at all to his heart. But then this light
slips down and charges this sin and this wrath upon
that very person, and shines so clearly in this charge
that the person cannot for his life deny it ("*You* are
this drunkard. *You* are that swearer."). And hereupon in the name of God arrests him with that
wrath which God has threatened to that sin and
sinner, and *now* the sinner begins to consider,
tremble, and break.

When Peter closed with the Jews and convinced
them that they in particular crucified Jesus Christ,
then their hearts were pricked. And when Nathan
drew his parable out of the cloud and unclothed his
message to David saying, "Thou art the man," *then*
David's heart began to break and take on. O see!
The subtle heart of man will endure and bear all the
historic notions of sin (as we can the names and na-
tures of diseases and medicines) without any aching
and sickness. But when the Lord brings down sin
from being a notion to being an obligation, and en-

ters an action against the soul within the soul, now,
and not before, the heart-workings and heart-break-
ings begin.

A conscience affliction. In respect of degrees and
quantity, this is in some more and in others less.
God's Spirit is an arbitrary agent in the gradual effects of bondage as well as in those gracious effects
of adoption. Nevertheless, though the degrees of
working are different, yet the work itself is certain.
The heart will never rightly be broken for sin till
conscience (which Bernard calls accuser, witness,
judge, and tormentor) begins to be awakened and
quickened. And believe it, if conscience, which has
been so stirred, begins to stir, if conscience, which
has been so often wounded, begins to wound, the
spirit of man will soon fail and break within him.

"Oh," says conscience, "what have you done to
thus provoke the holy and righteous and great God?
I know the several acts of your sinnings, and times,
and places, and persons, and circumstances, and I
have sad news to tell you. That great God against
whom you have so much and so often sinned, has
commanded and deputed me not only to speak no
peace, but also to speak His wrath and displeasure
unto you. And in His name I charge upon you all
your sins and all His just wrath revealed against
them."

And now the proud and stout heart of a sinner
begins to throb and fear and tremble. He thinks
that every threatening which he reads is a cloud of
tempests against him. He thinks that every judgment he hears of another is a sword drawn to cut
him also. He thinks that all the hell and torments

thereof mentioned in the Scriptures will ere long be his portion. And upon this his distracted soul cries out, "Oh, that I might never be! If I should die now, good Lord, what will become of me? If I should yet live, will the Lord ever be merciful to me? The sins which I see are many; the wrath which I feel is great, and that which I fear is infinite. If I live, I see I am an accursed creature; and if I die (O let me not die!), I fear I shall be forever a damned sinner (Oh, my soul breaks at that endless word of misery "forever.").

But yet this sinner cries out, "Lord! Lord! Is there no mercy, no hope of any mercy for me, a most vile sinner?"

With these mind-racking thoughts, away hastens this burdened, broken sinner into his closet. He shuts the door and down he falls on his knees. With much confusion of thoughts and fears he spreads all his sinnings before God, confessing one and then another, and then, with fervent agonies, he begs the Lord for more than his life: "Mercy, Lord! Mercy, mercy for a lost sinner, for a heinous sinner, for an undone sinner! Canst Thou pardon me? Wilt Thou pardon me? O Lord, pardon me! O Lord, be reconciled to me. Oh that I might have any hopes, the least hopes that Thou wouldest be merciful unto me!"

And now up rises this sinner with these or the like thoughts: "Well! I will read my Bible. I will hear such a minister. I will open my condition unto him and confer and inquire whether there is no balm in Gilead; whether there is a mercy seat, a city of refuge to entertain such a sinner as I am." And after awhile, upon careful search, he finds that yet there is hope, that there is an immeasurable sufficiency in the blood of Christ, and an ocean of full and free grace in God, and that God, not withstanding all his former sinnings against Him, is most willing and ready to accept him into mercy if he is willing to forsake his sins and embrace a Mediator.

The Formal Ingredients

Hereupon follows the second principal working which formally makes up evangelical contrition. It is *pudor* and *dolor*: shame and grief. Such kindness from the mercy seat makes him now as Ephraim, confounded and ashamed, and his heart to break into most melting floods of tears that ever he should be so monstrously vile to offend such tender and gracious bowels of mercy, which he now apprehends yearning towards him in and through Christ. As before, the apprehensions of divine wrath distracted and shivered him, so now the apprehensions of divine love totally dissolve and melt him. Though there were not heaven hereafter to crown him, yet he must grieve; and though there were not hell hereafter to burn him, yet he must exceedingly mourn for sinning against such a God.

This is that right evangelical contrition which I press for at this time! It is called in Scripture a softness of heart, a contrite heart, a mourning, a bitter mourning, and a great mourning, like that of Hadad Rimmon in the Valley of Megiddon (Zechariah 12:11). Ambrose calls it a heart melting and dissolving. Jerome calls it an exceeding lamenting. St. Augustine calls it a very heavy grief.

The Casuists and Schoolmen affirm it to be the greatest of all sorrows:

In conatu: The whole soul seems to send springs into it out of every faculty.

In extensione: It is a spring which, in this life, more or less, is continually dripping.

In appreciatione: The changed soul ever judges that a good God offended should be the prime cause of the greatest sorrow. And, lastly,

In intensione: For intention of displeasure in the will, there being no other thing with which or for the will is more displeased with itself than for sinning against God. And therefore, some of the Schoolmen propound this question, whether there should be more grief for sin than for the passion of Christ. Resolve it affirmatively: there is more cause of grief for sinning than for the death of Christ, because in the death of Christ there was something that pleased God (so far as it was a redemption), but there is nothing in sin which is not altogether displeasing unto God, considered formally as sin.

The Consequent Working

This rather shows and declares, then, what makes a broken heart—and it is hatred of sin. The heart which is rightly broken is not only broken *for* sin, but also *from* sin by a double hatred:

A hatred of abomination, loathing it as the greatest evil. Isaiah 30:22: "Get thee hence," say they.

A hatred of enmity and irreconciliation. "What have I to do any more with idols," said Ephraim in Hosea 14:8.

Thus you have heard what the breaking up of the fallow ground, or sinful heart, is. Now I proceed to demonstrate that it is the means to prevent the breaking down of a sinful nation. This may evidently appear:

1. By the finger of God in Scripture pointing a people to this work so that they might not sink into ruin, but be preserved. Read Ezekiel 18:30–31 and Joel 2:13–14.

2. By the pledges which God makes in several promises that if a sinful nation will take this course He will then spare them and continue them. Read Jeremiah 18:7–8 and 2 Chronicles 7:14.

3. By the records or instances of God's sparing a people, and a revoking of His wrath and judgments when they have set upon this heart-breaking course. Read Jonah 3:6–10 and 2 Chronicles 34:27.

4. By the executions of destruction because they would not hearken to this course. See 2 Chronicles 36:15–17.

QUESTION. But why should the breaking up of sinful hearts be a means to prevent the breaking down of a sinful nation? The reasons are these:

First, because where hearts are rightly broken for sins, there sins are pardoned. And where sins are pardoned, all breaking down is unquestionably prevented. In Isaiah you read of washing and cleansing (they are the same as this heart-breaking and mourning), and immediately you read of pardon. "Though your sins be as scarlet, they shall be as white as snow." And immediately after that you read of "eating the good of the land," a comfortable fruition of themselves and their country, and of all means and blessings.

Beloved, when sins are pardoned, then:

1. All their guilty clamor is silenced. Pardoned sins are disabled sins. They can bring no action against us. Debts forgiven shall never prejudice nor hurt us. Sins unpardoned can raise all the armies of God in heaven and earth against sinners, but once pardoned they are of no force or strength at all.

2. When sins are pardoned, all good has a free passage. God is reconciled and mercies have their commission to attend us. Now, says the Lord, "I will hear the heavens, and they shall hear the earth, and the earth shall hear the corn, and the wine and the oil, and they shall hear Jezreel," Hosea 2:21–22.

Second, if sinful hearts are broken, God has His end, and then all quarrels cease between Him and a nation. The Lord does not threaten destruction to a people for destruction's sake, but for humiliation's sake. Not that they may be destroyed, but that they should repent and *not* be destroyed.

Third, broken hearts are a wonderful delight unto the Lord. There are some things in which God has no delight. He has no delight in sinnings, Psalm 5:4, nor in punishments, Ezekiel 18:32. And there are two hearts in which God takes much delight, namely, in an upright heart and in a contrite heart. The broken heart He will not despise, nay, He will look upon that heart to revive it. If broken hearts are God's delight, and the objects of His reviving, then without question they are a means to prevent destruction.

Fourth, and last, when hearts are broken for sins,

then God's heart (if I may so phrase it) is broken with compassion unto sinners. Though sinners remain obstinate, yet divine compassions work strongly towards them. "How shall I give thee up, Ephraim? How shall I deliver thee, O Israel?" Hosea 11:8. What bowels then do you think are working in God when sinners are broken and humbled and turning? If God can so hardly find the way to punish impenitent Ephraim, will He not find the way to spare a humbling Ephraim? See Jeremiah 31:18: "I have surely heard Ephraim lamenting himself." And verse 20: "My bowels are troubled for him, I will surely have mercy upon him, saith the Lord."

Application

I have done with the explication of the point. I now address myself to the application of it, first, to all of us, and, second, to you of public employment.

Is the breaking up of sinful hearts the means to prevent the breaking down of a sinful nation? Then let every one of us here search and try the temper and frame of our hearts, whether they are broken or unbroken. Beloved, I beseech you sadly to consider a few things:

1. Brokenness of heart is the work of this day. This is a day of humiliation, but what is a humbling day without a humbled heart? To present yourselves before the great God at such a time with all your sins, and yet without hearts broken for those sins, is not only an irreligious incongruity, but also a high provocation of our God. It is like Zimri's act when all the congregation were "weeping before the door

of the tabernacle" in Numbers 25:6.

Come we not this day with all sorts of guilt upon our souls, and with ropes about our necks, expecting (if the Lord should render unto us our deserts) the sentence of death, and confess as much, and yet dare we play the hypocrite, having hearts utterly un-broken under all this?

2. Brokenness of heart is the hope of this day. I profess seriously unto you that, were you as much in fasting as John's disciples, and in praying as much as Christ's disciples, could you by fasting make your knees to faint and your flesh to fail, and resolve your bodies into a very skeleton, yet if your hearts were not broken for your sins, neither your selves, nor your endeavors, nor our own nation, nor the dis-tressed Church of Ireland, nor any other would be the better for it. As one of the fathers said of learn-ing, "All learning is suspected, nay, disrespected by me, wherein is not the mention of Christ." That I may affirm of all solemn fastings whatsoever: the Lord regards them not if the broken heart is not found in them.

What Joseph said to his brethen, "unless you bring your brother Benjamin with you, you shall not see my face", or, as Isaac said to his father, "Behold the fire and the wood, but where is the lamb for a burnt offering?" that the Lord says unto us: "Fast as often as you please, and pray too; but unless your hearts are broken for your sins, nothing that you do shall find favor with Me. All the rest is as wood and fire; the lamb, the sacrifice of a contrite heart, which is what I look at and for, is wanting."

"Get thee behind me," said Jehu to the several

messengers, "what have you to do with peace?" Confessions and prayers are the messengers of our souls to God, but unless the sinful heart is broken, they will never be messengers of peace.

If any of you would angle in a river, would you throw in a naked line only? Would this be to any purpose? Sirs, I know well that if a fast is rightly performed, it has as many promises of blessings and mercies (see Isaiah 58) as any religious duty whatsoever. Nay, and I think that you never read in all the Bible, nor yet find in any experience, of its right performance without some sudden and remarkable testimony of God's gracious acceptance and answer. But then breaking of hearts ever accompanied those prevailing and victorious fasts, as you may read in Judges, Samuel, the Kings, Ezra, and Nehemiah. And, for my part, I would not scruple the affection of any convenient mercy, nor the diversion of any impending evil, if once, with all our fastings, there was also a breaking up of our fallow grounds. If God could in this command our hearts, we might, then, in some sense, command our God.

3. Have we not, all of us, sufficient cause to break our sinful hearts? Should sins, should calamities abroad, should dangers at home break hearts? All these may then work upon us. Our sins have broken the heart of Christ, and are such as have broken off God from a people, and have broken many churches down. Can you be ignorant of the professed idolatry in this land? of the horrid blasphemies? of the overflowing drunkenness? or the Sabbath's profanation? And if we look at calamities abroad, why, as Jacob said, Joseph is not, and Simeon is not, so we may say,

Bohemia is broken up, and the Palatinate is broken
up, and Ireland is breaking up, and yet the hearts of
sinful England will not be broken up? Nay, look at
the dangers hovering like a cloud over this land,
and dropping already in manifold and sundry divisions, in manifold plots, in manifold and several
contradictions, and even ready to break forth (O
Lord, let it not break forth) in a bitter internal war
among ourselves, where every man's sword shall be
against his brother, and the child may kill the parent or the parent kill his child (bowels sheathed in
bowels), no man is scarcely secure in his own family! Our sins are bringing this upon us, and yet our
hearts will not break for those sins. The God of all
wisdom and mercy break our hearts so that this
judgment *may* not do that which all our foreign enemies *could* not do, break down our church and nation.

4. And if judgments should break in upon sinners before hearts are broken for sins, good Lord!
What, where are they? Dudulius relates a sad story of
Bochna, a woman who had but two sons. While she
was walking with the one towards the river, she
heard the other crying out. Hastening back, she
found a knife sticking in him which killed him
quickly. Then she returned to her other child thinking to solace herself in her only child, but he, in her
absence, had fallen into the river and drowned—
both lost at once. Ah, sirs! We have but two children:
a soul and a body! What a heavy loss will it be to lose
both these at once! To be cut off by an angry enemy
and to be cast off by a mighty God! To lose a life
and, at the same time, to lose an eternal life! To lose

safety and salvation at once! 'Tis true that if a sinner's heart is broken by grace, there is no question of mercy; but when an impenitent sinner's life is broken by judgment, his hopes are gone.

5. We shall assuredly be broken off if we are not broken up. Beloved, there are two vile malignities in an unbroken heart:

First, it is one of the greatest spiritual judgments. Said a reverend man once, "If I must be put to my option, I would rather be in hell with a sensible heart than live on earth with a reprobate mind." So I say, a hardened and unbroken heart is, in some respects, a judgment worse than hell, forasmuch as one of the greatest sins is far greater in evil than any of the greatest punishments.

Second, it is the immediate and unavoidable forerunner of the greatest of temporal judgments. "He that hardens his heart shall be destroyed suddenly and that without remedy," Proverbs 29:1. Observe that place: there is no less than destruction, which is not a particular and imperfect damage; but it is a complete ruin, and this destruction is certain. Note that it is "shall," not "may perhaps" be destroyed. But when? Suddenly! Aye, but will not the sinner shift it off and withstand it? No, but he shall be destroyed without remedy. His destructions shall not be prevented. You may read all this in the old world, and in Pharoah, and in the Jews before the Babylonian captivity, and afterwards in the Roman devastation which lasted these 1600 years.

6. But now where are our broken hearts? I know not what to say. My heart breaks within me. Oh, that it could be broken because hearts are generally un-

broken. Sinners are secure; consciences are seared; wickedness is bold; sins are a delight and a pastime. God is neither seen nor feared in His judgments, in His warnings, in His dealings. Reformation is abhorred. Most do not know what humiliation for sin is; and, if they do know, they find it distasteful. Serious thoughts of our sinful ways—who takes them up? Sufficient time for self-examination—who takes it for himself? Every man runs on in his course, loves as he did before and lives as he did before, and never knew a trouble in his soul, nor a tear in his eye either for his own sin or for the sins of others all his days. And what will the end of all this be?

O that God would pity us this day, and break our hearts for us, though it is so irksome and contrary to our flesh and blood. It is better, said one of the Fathers, to die one death than to live and fear all deaths. It is better to suffer the heart to be broken than to expose ourselves to all sorts of judicial and eternal breakings. "O Lord," said dying Fulgen, "make me a penitent sinner, and then let me find an indulgent Father."

Never look for great mercies, for long mercies, for any mercies with unbroken hearts. We are no good; we can do no good; we can expect no good till our sinful hearts are broken. Oh, Christians, be persuaded this day to get broken hearts! God can do it for you, and will do it for you, if you will but use the means and seek Him. Take spare time to study the law, to study conscience, to study the gospel, to study mercies, to study judgments, to study Christ, to study all, that after all our hearts may be broken for our sins, that God may not break away from us, but continue to be our God, and that judgments, which look so black upon us may be broken off, and plots contrived against us may break asunder, and all spiritual and earthly mercies may break down in mercy upon us.

And thus much is spoken with respect unto every one who hears me this day.

I have besides all this a particular errand from God to you who are public persons and have summoned me this day unto this public work. I think that the Lord speaks to you in some respect what He once spoke to the prophet Jeremiah in chapter 1:10: "See, I have this day set you over the nations, and over the kingdoms, to root out, and to pull down, and to destroy, and to throw down."

And blessed be the Lord, and blessed be your souls, and blessed be your endeavors, that notwithstanding the infinite difficulty of the work and the malignant contrariety you meet with, yet your hearts are undaunted and resolved to finish the work, as honorable as Parliament ever undertook, and as profitable to Church and State as ever Christians enterprised. Your armies shall be made strong by the blessing of the everlasting God of Jacob, let popish and malevolent and ignorant persons say or do what they can.

Give me leave, first, to represent unto you some public plots of fallow ground which you, blessed be God, have begun to break. Nevertheless, they need yet a more full breaking up. And, second, to present in all humble fidelity unto you some few intimations and directions.

The public plots of fallow ground which need breaking up are especially four:

1. The first lies directly in the Valley of Hinnom, and it is idolatry—a piece of ground which lies too much in every shire of this land. What county is there where much popery is not? Sirs! You must break this ground up or it will break our land up. There is not such a God-provoking sin, a God-removing sin, a Church-dissolving sin, a kingdom-breaking down sin as idolatry. The soul of God abhors it. Down with it! Down with it even to the ground!

2. The second lies near to Beth-Aven, and it is superstition, which is but a bawd to gross idolatry. A rise in practice, even now, notwithstanding all that you have said and done, as if a Parliament had never opened a mouth against it. If a due and careful inquiry were made, I do not doubt but you shall find in too many churches and public places as many altars, and as many crucifixes hanging over them, and as many tapers on altars, and as much bowing towards the east and the altar almost as much as when you began this Parliament.

3. The third lies just upon the coasts of Egypt, that land of darkness, and it is ignorance. This is a very large circuit of ground. There are many, many places of this land which lie fallow to this day; never any husbandman nor plow have entered in to break up those grounds. What a lamentable thing that, since Jesus Christ came into the world, and since the gospel came to this land, after several scores of years, how many parishes in Wales, and in the North, and in other counties there are which

scarcely have enjoyed this much mercy as to hear one solid soul-working sermon concerning Christ and salvation by Him! O sirs! Let your hearts bleed in pity to these poor souls. Liberties, I confess, are precious, and so are our estates, and so are our bodies and lives. Oh, then, what are souls? What are precious souls which cost the most precious blood of the Lord Jesus Christ?

4. The fourth ill plot of ground lies on Mizpah, or, if you please, on Mount Tabor, "for there the priests were a net and a snare," Hosea 5:1. And this is an idle and evil ministry. Sirs! Mistake me not. I speak not of our ministers indefinitely. I know that we have as godly, as learned, as painful, and as profitable ministers as any in all the Christian world, but I speak only of such whose special gifts consist in one or two things: either quietly to read out of a book, and to discreetly gather up their tithes, or malevolently to discountenance all godliness and rail against the Parliament.

Ah, worthy sirs! It would amaze any ingenious man to travel such a country as England, and, passing through many parishes, discover that this, after all, is his diurnal; the patron is popish; the minister is an idle dunce, or else a drunkard, or a swearer, or else a scoffer, preaching all holiness out of his pulpit, out of his church, out of his family, out of his parish. And his people are like him and love to have it so.

And thus what? Between the idle minister and the evil minister, the poor people never come to knowledge, or, without which knowledge never come to anything, they never come to the love and practice of any saving good. These are the principle fallow grounds in this land which need our cares and pains.

Now follow the intimations and directions which I humbly present unto you.

1. Break them up. If ever you will quit your own souls, and the trust reposed in you, and the whole land of judgments spiritual and corporeal, if you ever desire to gain ground in your public intentions for good, for the Lord's sake break up these fallow grounds.

But then, in the next place, go very deep with your plow or else you will never break up these grounds—the deeper the better. As all good is most strengthened, so all evil is most crushed in its causes. Take heed of shallow work and surface plowing. God's eyes are upon you, and so are the eyes of judicious men who can distinguish between scraping and breaking. Our misery will be but finely laid to sleep awhile if your plow does not go deep.

Does a little cringing move you? Oh, then, let gross idolatry beat and burn your souls! Does boldness in a questioned minister displease you? Oh, then, let his gross wickedness stir you utterly to disburden poor people's souls of him. Oh, let sad complaints have quick and full redress!

And go over the fallow grounds which you have broken; go over them again. Yea, and again! Fallow grounds must often be broken up with the plow. Even the actions of the most judicious receive more ripeness by review. By often doing we grow into a better acquaintance with what is to be done. Our

first doings are rather trials and enterprises; the
second doings ever prove the work.

Besides that, our affections also are oftentimes
too quick for our eyes. The desires of doing some
good may outrun the due search of much evil. Add
yet further that ingrained diseases are not easily
stirred, much less destroyed by one potion. Evils
long in gathering, and much baked into and settled
in a state or church, are not so suddenly cured as
vulgar people in their haste imagine. Shall I speak
one more thing? There is as much art almost as sin,
as much guilt as guiltiness. The laws are ingenuous,
but offenders are fraudulent and subtle. Sirs! You
deal with bold offenders, and with cunning offenders too, which, if you look not the better to it, will
quite delude and frustrate all your religious and pious intentions.

Shall I tell you what I know, and what the country
sighs and sheds tears at, that notwithstanding your
religious pity to their souls, yet their souls are as
much abused as ever. They have complained of some
ill ministers. You hearken unto them, but in the
meantime the minister exchanges his living with
another, perhaps, afar off, unknown to the people,
against whom there can be, for the present, no legal
exception. And thus they perish still for lack of
bread.

Therefore, worthy sirs, out with your plow again.
You are by all these after-works much more directed
how to manage and carry on your work.

Last, be as earnest and active as you possibly can
to send laborers into the field, to plant all the land
with a heart-breaking ministry. All will come to

nothing unless this is done. Pluralities are voted down, but what good will that be when all comes to this? Before that order, one bad man had two good livings, and now two bad men have each of them one too good for them both. I will say no more unto you, but be serious and courageous in this work in settling a good ministry, with which join also an answerable magistrate. To do this is your duty; this is your honor; this will be our safety and happiness; this will be your great reward in heaven.

Go on thus in this breaking work and prosper. There is no man ever did anything for God and lost by it, or to His Church but who gained by it. If you will go on with a humble and unwearied zeal, it shall shortly be said of this Parliament, "These were Scotland's umpire, Ireland's guard and revenge, England's preservation, the Church's safety, and religion's glory."

And so I pass from the plow to the seed, from the plowing up of fallow grounds to the sowing of them being broken up, expressed with its caution in the text: "And so not among thorns."

PART TWO
"And sow not among thorns."

That breaking up the ground must go before sowing, and that a sowing must follow the breaking up, is no question to a judicious man. For as it would be a vain thing to sow when the ground is not broken up (the seed would be but a prey), so it would be as foolish when the ground is broken up not to sow (the labor would never prove a harvest), breaking up the ground being in itself only a work for another work. And indeed, as the historian spoke of the emperor, that he rather lacked vice than was virtuous, so it may be said of a person and a nation if their fallow grounds are broken up and yet not sown, they are rather not wicked than good. For negatives alone make no estate to be gracious. It must be some positive quality which gives perfection and denomination.

They say well in philosophy that while the motion is passing from the *terminus a quo*, it is but *fieri*, and till the *terminus ad quem* is attained, it is not in *facto esse;* the work is but on the way—it is not at the end nor done. The same is true in divinity, for cessation from evil is not sufficient without an operation of good. To pull down wickedness is not enough unless we also set up godliness. Josiah pulled down idols, but then he likewise restored and set up the true worship of God. Our Savior not only corrected the false glosses wherewith the Pharisees had corrupted the law, but also erected and established the true sense and genuine interpretation of it. Jehu to this day lies under the tongue and censure of

hypocrisy, notwithstanding all his zeal against Baal
and the priests, because, after all this, "He took no
care or heed to walk in the Law of the Lord God of
Israel with all his heart." It is, I think, a true maxim
that all true quarrels with evil arise from the love of
good; and, therefore, the defacings and displacings
of the former ought to end in the advancings and
settlings of the latter. And verily, it would be a
weaker design to undo the one and yet not to do the
other.

First, because moral evils will not be cured but by
contrary qualities. A state will warp about for awhile
to its corruptions, if care is not taken for its perfecting and preservation too, just like water will slip
back to coldness even though it was heated for a
time.

Second, though a nation is somewhat less miserable because evil is removed, yet it will not be happy
till good is planted. You shall find, besides this, that
the soul of the public state will answer that of the
person. As the presence of what oppresses a man is a
burden, so the absence of what is convenient will
certainly prove a complaint. Both religion and nature instruct us in this. Religion puts men on for
holiness as well as pulls men off from sinfulness.
And nature has engrafted in it not only depths of
distastes against apprehended evils, but also vast desires for all thoroughly apprehended good. Neither
will it receive satisfaction in the one without the
other. Yea, ordinary policy can discern as great an
aptness to tumult where convenience is withheld as
there is to impatience where misery is felt.

Shall I add one thing more? In all public

changes and alterations, these ever go in the
thoughts of the vulgar, confident expectations that
some other thing must succeed in the place of any
thing that is removed (especially in matters of religion where corruption is discerned on all sides), the
ordination and plantation of which, if public authority does not take in hand, you shall find that ordinary heads will presume to do. And what confusion it will make among people, and future difficulties to yourselves, I leave to your religious wisdoms to
consider.

So, then, it is evident that a sowing ought to follow the breaking up. Yet any kind of sowing is not a
sufficient consequence. The direction is given in
the text with a caution: "Sow, but do not sow among
thorns."

Interpreters abound in their opinions concerning these thorns. Chrysostom understands these to
be idols, entangling and piercing as the sharpest of
briars and thorns. Origen and Jerome understand
these briars to be covetousness and the cares of the
world, which likewise are scratching and wounding.
Others understand them to be all our sinful corruptions. There are thorns in our hearts, said Bernard,
as well as in our fields. And some understand the
thorns to be mixtures of worship crept into the worship of God among the Jews, as do Sanctius and
others. But with the favor of all these, and yet with
submission, I conjecture that these words are a
proverbial speech and suggest only this to us: that as
the Jews were to break down what was evil in themselves and the Church and State, so they were to set
upon the doing of all good in private and public in

such a manner and order that their pains and endeavors might not come to nothing, but be to some
good purpose indeed.

A husbandman who sows will sow that he may
reap, and not lose his seed and labor, and therefore
will not sow among thorns. This would be an improper work, and would prove utterly unprofitable. It
is a thousand to one if ever his seed comes up, for
thorns have a stealing, withdrawing, and frustrating
quality; or, if it does come up, yet it will be lost. It
cannot be gathered; there is no coming at it with
sycthe or sickle. Thorns have a hindering malignity
as well as a stifling power.

DOCTRINE 2. From this exposition, I observe
this second doctrine: **All penitential and reforming
work must be so managed and acted that it may not
prove a vain and fruitless work, but may come to be a
successful and profitable work.** It must not be a sowing among thorns, but such a sowing which may in
the issue produce a harvest. It is as good to have
never a whit as have never the better.

You read in Scripture of many sowers:

1. The evil man sowed tares. We have read of late
many such sowers, not only professed priests and
Jesuits, but also some among ourselves who have
sown popish, Arminian, Socinian, and superstitious
tares.

2. The cunning man sows divisions and dis-
sentions. There have been, and still are, too many
who sow division between the King and the
Parliament, between ministers and ministers, between ministers and people, and between people
and people.

3. The foolish man sows and cares not what (in respect of the seed), nor where (in respect of the soil), nor when (in respect of the time), and so all is lost and comes to nothing.

4. The wise man in his sowing looks to the seed that it is good and clean, and to the soil, that it is prepared right, and to the season, that it is fit, upon which, through God's blessing, the seed sown takes root, prospers, and proves a harvest.

Of this I now speak in the proposition which, whether you limit it to a repentance that is personal, or extend it to a reformation that is national, holds true in both. And the text will bear both. The one and the other must be so dispersed that it may not prove vain and lost, but effectual and successful.

Sirs! Though penitential works rightly done are never without success and blessing, yet pretendingly penitential agents may so carry on these works (materially good) that they may never prove formally and eventually good or beneficial. And therefore you read in Scripture that many prayings and fastings and solemn meetings and tears and other doings have found no acceptance with God, nor wrought any subjective alterations in persons, nor change from misery to mercy in a nation. Read the Prophets concerning the Jews, and that will be sufficient testimony.

In six cases they prove to be nothing but a sowing among thorns:

1. *When they are but external, not acted by any inward principles, the effects rather of art and parts than of the heart and grace.* They are shells, not kernels; tears of the eyes, but not tears of the heart; prayers of the lips,

but not prayers of the soul. They are shadows and pageants of repentance, seeming to be so to the eye of man, but not heart-workings which only are interpreted to be true and solid to the eye of God.

The swan in the Law was white in feathers, yet reputed unclean and unfit for sacrifice because the skin under those feathers was black. Religious workings stand in God's account according to the quality of the workman, the heart of whom is all in all for acceptance or rejection. God reputes nothing done which the heart does not. Art may take man more than nature, but not with God; the more art, the less acceptance. A painted repentance which is only external will do ourselves and the nation as much good as a painted sword, as a painted staff, and as a painted fire. That will not cut; this will not help; and the other will not heat. And no more will a merely external repentance prevent any judgments or obtain any mercies.

2. *When they are but partial.* A putting down of some sins and a keeping up of other sins will be as vain as to cure the palsey and yet to neglect the plague, or as to mend the pump and neglect the leak. Jehu's golden calves made an end of him, though he made an end of Baal's images and priests. And so in the doing of good, it will come to nothing, though some good is done, if the best good is neglected. The Pharisees did many acts of righteousness, but lost them and themselves because they opposed and rejected Christ, who was the chief and only righteousness.

There is, beloved, such a natural union between all vices (and so there is among virtues) that they (in a formal working) ever include a universal hatred or universal love. No man can be thought to be good who is at defiance with any known particular good; nor does he cease to be wicked who does not hate and oppose every known evil. Particular and exclusive actings in the one and the other serve only to the disacceptance of the works, and to the greater condemnation of the persons. Though imbecility shall never be any prejudice to our works, yet subtlety and partiality shall.

3. *When they are but circumstantial.* Though a multitude of lesser evils is crushed, if yet the greater are spared to survive this reformation will prove like Saul's discretion with the Amalekites, who spared the fattest and destroyed the poorest; but he lost the kingdom by it.

Circumstantial reformations, I grant, are more easy and quick, but those which are most deep are ever most safe. A cloth will stop the wound as soon, and perhaps sooner, than the plaster, but the plaster, which searches to the quick, heals much better. If the tree is stark naught and good for no service, it is better to cut it down to the root than to hire men many days to cut off the limbs.

There are three great mischiefs in all circumstantial and slight acts:

One is the greatest causes of wrath are not met with.

A second is that in a short time all the intertwined evils will, by a new influence from their roots, sprout up again.

The third is that when these evils once feel their strength and regain their opportunity they will become more evil and mischievous than ever. Histories and experiences witness enough of this. Popery was hot in former kings' times, but when it got out the bit by the death of Edward VI, it burst out with more burnings and flaming cruelty in Queen Mary's days.

4. *When they are only co-active.* I mean such actings unto which there is little or no concurrence of a judicious and active will, but are rather the sparkles which are forced out by the collision of flints, elicited rather by the impressions of appearing and urging evils—like Pharaoh's obedience which was forced out of judgments and nothing else.

Mariners in a storm are very pious, but in a calm turn as wicked as before. The Jews in their straits were as pliable as could be desired. They would part with anything and do anything for God; but when the sun arose, this vain cloud and dew were gone and scattered. If a cloud of wrath is that which puts us on to be and to do good, a few beams of temporal safety will find us flat and strangers again. The acts of men spring sometimes from fear and sometimes from love; those of fear may be more strong and stirring for the present (like a flood which runs more violently than a river), but those of love are most acceptable and constant. Voluntary acts, though sometimes more slow, yet are at all times more successful. In the gospel, John ran faster than Peter, yet, being at the sepulcher, Peter went farther than John. John looked down, but Peter *went* down. An arrow flies swifter and a man walks slower, yet a man may sooner walk to the mark than the arrow can hit it. Sirs! No private or public work of reformation will come to good which is derived only from a fear of evil and not from a love of good. When the circumstances of evil are of such, the evil heart will show itself evil again.

5. *When they are hypocritical and vainglorious, done by ourselves and for ourselves.* It is a strange thing to observe how the spirits of men are balanced and mounted and kept parallel with the ends which they propound unto themselves! The art and strength and length of our workings are ever molded in our own aims and respects. One man acts for God, another acts for himself. The works of the one are blessed and proper; the attempts of the other quickly languish and are blasted. As vicious acts are under God's curse, so vainglorious acts are out of His blessing. Sincerity, humble sincerity, is that which gives life, finds acceptance, and is crowned with success.

If a man in his religious performances of praying, fasting, and humbling himself should seek not God but himself, as the Pharisees did, his vainglory would purchase only the applause of men and rejection with God. All his works will be lost and come to nothing. "Verily, you have your reward," said Christ. A poor reward to have breath for breath! And so, in public attempts, if you should not entirely seek God, His glory, His truth, His worship, but yourselves, your work will never prosper. It will rest only on your own parts to act it, and on your own strength to consumate and perfect it; and what blessed issue can be expected where weak man is left alone to be the author and finisher of great actions?

6. *When they are fickle and inconstant.* They are be-

gun, perhaps, with some fervency, but then laid
aside by as much tempidity; an anguished zeal: hot
in attempting, but cold in effecting; one day to act
like penitents, and the next day to live like sinners:
one time humbling and praying, and after awhile
cursing and swearing. Sometimes we offer all our
service and strength for Christ and religion, and
then are suddenly intent only to our own delights
and ways, forgetting (like those who are much in
complements) all our zeal and professions. What a
vanity will this prove to be? What harvest will ensue
when the husbandman will one hour sow a handful
of seed, and a week later go home and do nothing!

It is observed in nature that many remiss acts
(which have no proportion to effects) and some
strong acts soon remitted will equally come to nothing. If there is too weak a strength in the root, or if
all the strength shoots out at once, little or not, no
fruit will follow. Yet this deceit cleaves much to
man's heart so that it will either be constantly bad
or else inconstantly good. It has some degrees of
heat to begin, but lacks that prudence of patient endeavor and coming to finish and perfect, like him
in the gospel who began to build but did not make
an end. From this results a vanity and successless-
ness to our works. The ripeness of which is betrayed
many times more by our own remissness than by
other's opposition. They stick and die in the birth
because we do not continue in our strength to help
and bring them forth.

I see that the time and your wearied patience call
upon me to hasten and finish. Give me leave to
make some useful application of all this, and then I

am done. The application shall be in this as in the former part, a word first to all of us, and then to you of great employment and public service.

Application

To Every One of Us

We stand here this day before the Lord, and seem to do the work of a solemn fast day. We confess our sins, we pray, we humble ourselves, and profess that we will repent and reform and obey the Lord! Here has been much seed sown (prayers are seed, tears are seed, and sermons are seed).

But if all this sowing should be but a sowing among thorns, if all this should be so managed by us that our prayers, that our confessions, that our hearings, that our resolvings should come to nothing and prove nothing; if after one, two, three, many humblings we should not be humbled; if after all the changes which befall our times our hearts are not changed, but sins remain as strong and judgments remain as near; if after all this God should not be reconciled unto us, our trangressions should not be pardoned, judgments should not be withdrawn, mercies should not be sent down, what a bitter and sad thing would this be, for a man to perish though he prays, and to be destroyed though he fasts, and a nation to be made a curse and a hissing and a desolation after it has seemed to meet the Lord by solemn confessions and humiliations! To perish in the shows of repentance is a bitter perishing.

It was a sad greeting which they found from

Christ. "Lord," they said, "we have heard Thee preaching in our synagogues. We have eaten and drank in Thy presence."

"Yet," said Christ to them, "depart from Me, ye workers of iniquity. Verily, I know you not."

So, when we come to die and then come to judgment, and say, "Lord, we have heard Thy Word. We have fasted; we have prayed; we have afflicted our bodies and souls." And yet Christ shall say, "Depart, I know you not. You heard My Word indeed, but you did not obey My Word. You confessed your sins, but you never forsook your sins. You did a little good, but you never became good. You professed obedience, but you never cared to walk in My ways. And therefore all that you have done shall never do you any good." Would this not be a sad and heavy answer to our self-deluded works?

Nay, put the case now: what if, after all our fastings, the same judgment (or worse) should befall us which befalls our poor brethren in Ireland, that the sword should break forth among us, and all the unmerciful and sudden calamities of war should beleaguer us, that in a moment the gospel should be banished, our liberties should be embondaged, our estates should be exhausted, our lands should be dispossesed, our houses should be burned, our coffers should be ransacked, our bodies should be tortured, and our lives should be threatened? Good Lord!

Would we say, "Has all our fasting and humbling come to this? We looked for good and not evil. We looked for peace and not destruction. Why has this happened?"

The Lord might answer us, "When did you fast to Me? And when did you pray to Me? Indeed, you prayed against judgments, but you would never leave your sins which, I told you often, would pull down judgments. You would have had mercies, but I could never persuade you to repent in good earnest. You trusted vain thoughts of your own, but you would never be humbled to purpose. You would sow among thorns, and see now what you got by it."

O Christian, think seriously on these things! God has called to England once, again, often a longer time: "Repent indeed! Turn from your evil ways indeed; be upright and holy indeed; walk with Me once at length in truth."

Judgments have called; warnings have called; consciences still call; dangers still call; fears still call; the ministers of God, like prophets of old, still call and cry and beseech and weep. Turn yet unto the Lord; turn not feignedly, but with all your hearts; sow not among thorns. Yet, Lord, who believes our reports and our calls? The prophet is reputed a fool and the spiritual man mad. Men will be sinful still. They will, perhaps one out of ten thousand, be seemingly penitent. And the issue, I fear, will be this: "The destruction of the transgressors and of the sinners shall be together," Isaiah 1:28. And "while they be folden together as thorns, they shall be devoured as stubble fully dry," Nahum 1:10.

But, sirs, let us yet be persuaded to repent and reform ourselves to purpose. If ever we purpose to repent, or would repent to purpose, this is the time. All within us, all without us, all abroad, and all at home beg it at our hearts. Oh, that God would work all His works in us so that our self-reforming work may begin, go on, hold out, and abound, and that God may be reconciled to us and this our sinful land.

To You of Public Employment
   Many excellent works are fallen into your hands. Some of them you have gone through with already, and more, we are persuaded, had received their seal had not the excellency of your attempts raised against you the enmity of manifold oppositions and contradictions. My humble and earnest entreaty of you is only this: let not those remaining excellent works (if it is possible, so much as in you lies) forever stick in the birth. Let them not die in mere intentions or propositions, but strive to bring them unto their due and much-desired perfection. You have begun some things:

1.   About erroneous doctrines.
2.   Against superstitious practices.
3.   Against idolatry, seducing priests, and Jesuits.
4.   With notorious delinquents and offenders.
5.   Against scandalous ministers and innovations.
6.   For the settling of a faithful and laborious ministry.
7.   For an honorable maintenance and encouragement of it. O never let us stand to the courtesy of the vulgar.
8.   For the easing of tender consciences.
9.   For the vindicating of the Lord's day.
10. For the settling of all distractions, and hopes

of a church reformation according to the Word of God, against which malice itself cannot justly open its mouth.

11.   For the succouring and relieving of poor and distressed Ireland. Hasten all that you can, lest it prove too late.

Now, God forbid, that such works as these should ever fall to the ground after so many years' misery, after so many thousand prayers, after so many gracious overtures which you have made. Let it not be said of you in these works as he said of his own, he was doing them, but they were never done.

Take up your first thoughts and engage your hearts and resolutions and all your endeavors speedily and successfully to carry on at least this one work of all works, a solid reformation. Believe me, it is the work which will bring a blessing upon all your other works. Peruse that place well in Haggai 2:18–19: "Consider now from this day, even from the day that the foundation of the Lord's Temple was laid, consider it. From this day I will bless you." Now Zerubbabel might reply, "We would set to this work, but we are afraid of warlike opposition." To this the Lord answers, in verses 22 and 23, "I will overthrow the throne of kingdoms, and I will destroy the strength of the kingdoms of the heathen; and I will overthrow the chariots, and the horses, and the riders. And I will take thee Zerubbabel My servant, and I will make thee as a signet. . . ." Look to that work, and I will assuredly look to your person and safeties.

Now, that you may effectually carry on all these great works (and especially that of Church reformation) so that all may be prosperous, and in the event come to something, make use of two directions which I humbly propound to you.

DIRECTION 1. Strip yourselves of all the things which will weaken your hearts and make your endeavors still slow and fruitless.

Therefore, first, put off your sins or else they will put off your work. Evil men are seldom apt for, or prove successful in, good attempts. There is nothing which intricates our actions more than our sins, which likewise ensnare our souls. Enterprises set upon, either without God or against God, are like arrows shot up aloft which never do good, but many times do much hurt. It is affirmed only of the godly man that "whatever he doth shall prosper," Psalm 1:3.

Second, you must put off irregular fears. You will never be exactly serviceable to God or religion if you have anything to lose. "Should such a man as I flee?" said Nehemiah in 6:11. Guilty persons who are contriving against the foundations of a church and state may well fear. Their consciences may read terrors, dangers, and losses to them; but persons royally summoned, and piously employed for the right settling of a church and kingdom, as their attempts are above all contumacy, so their hearts should be above all fancies and fears. "If ye be followers of that which is good, who is he that will harm you?" There can never be any true danger nor loss by being good or doing good in our callings. The King of Poland, when his servant Zelislaus lost his hand in the wars, sent him instead thereof a golden hand. You shall never expend your strength for God in vain. His service is good and His reward is sure.

Third, you must put off favors. As a public man should have nothing to lose, so he should have nothing to get. He should be above all price or sale. Truth and public good should only sway and command him. He has too impotent a spirit whose services (like the dial) must be set only by the sun, who says to advancement and respect, as Tiberius once answered Justinius (though upon a better ground and end): "I am only thy clay and wax."

It was a brave commendation of Luther (though not intended by the Cardinal who spoke it): "That German beast cares not for gold." Henry, afterwards Duke of Saxony, rather adventured the hopes of the dukedom than that he would be bound not to change and reform a corrupt religion.

Fourth, you must put off prejudices. If the great work of church reformation seems to any of you either sordid or contemptible, or hopeless or impossible, or needless and idle, or unseasonable and inconvenient, you will either be formal in attempts, subtle to entange, or professedly opposite so as to crutch the work, and you will bring it to nothing. But yet, worthies of our Israel, know that:

Reformation is an honorable work. It is a work fit for God, fit for the greatest monarchs on earth; and the greatest reformers in religion have attained thereby to the greatest splendor and glory, as Hezekiah, Jehosophat, Josiah, and King Edward.

Reformation is a possible work. Though there are many knots and blocks and rubs and alarms, yet you must unanimously and strenuously act. Act and the work is done. The historians ascribe most of

King Alexander's success to his courage; there was nothing he attempted but he conceived it might be done. All works for God are both honorable and feasible. Tertullian, comparing the resurrection with creation, said it was more easy to make up the body again than simply to make it to be. The same holds true in this case: it is more easy to reform than to form a church. It is easier work to cure a diseased body than to enliven a dead body.

Reformation is a needful work. A reformation is needful when a church is likely to be poisoned with errors, or to be rent with contrariety of opinions, or is sick with manifold corruptions. This is our condition, and, besides, all this, we see great judgments hanging over us which have befallen other churches. Would it not be better to reform *before* judgments than *under* them? Who can tell but it may be an effectual means to prevent them.

Last, reformation is a seasonable work. If you judge a fit season for our church to be humbled, assuredly, then, it is a fit season for it to be reformed. That which puts us upon the one directs us also to the other. But I pass on.

DIRECTION 2. If you would carry on this work for good, then you must get into your hearts and cherish in your thoughts all those things which will quicken you to the perfecting of such a work.

First, you must labor to possess your hearts with those active, industrious, and unwearied graces of self-denial, of ardent love to God, of enflamed zeal for His glory, and of sublime faith, which will raise your spirits above all difficulties and oppositions, above all clouds and seas. Were men thus qualified,

they would then count nothing too dear or too
much for God, but would most cheerfully spend and
be spent for Him. They would lend all their honors,
places, gifts, abilities, all to the service of Christ.

Second, you must cherish quickening thoughts. I
will make bold to propound some unto you, only to
add at least to what you have and already know.

1. Mind the dignity of the work, and mind little
the malignity of the opposers. When the temple was
to be rebuilt, you know what opposition Sanballat
and Tobiah and others made, what accusations,
what letters, what attempts and devices against
Zerubbabel and the rest. But they minded the work
of the temple the more; their eyes were upon God
and His service. So, when Luther began the Reformation in Germany, you read that the Pope and his
Cardinals, and their curs presently opened their foul
mouths, crying out that he was a liar, treacherous,
an apostate, a trumpet of rebellion and sedition, and
that all which Luther had charged on the Pope were
his own vain surmises and devices. Yet Luther went
on with the work and, in spite of all contradiction,
prevailed and prospered.

The same we read in our own chronicles. When
King Edward set upon reformation, what scorns,
derisions, oppositions, sides, tumults encountered
by the friars and the popish party did he endure! Yet
he kept on at the work and greatly prospered in it.
The excellency of his work, a consciousness of his
duty, and confidence in God made his ark to swim
upon all those raging waters.

2. Mind your encouragements more and all discouragements less. Empedocles once said, "Take

away heaven and I am nobody." All serenity comes from above us. The damps rise from that which should be under our feet. Worthy sirs, as the prophet's chariots with him were more than the chariots of the adversaries against him, so, I may say, there are more with you (being in God's work) than can be against you. In a good work you have a God commanding you (as once to Joshua in Joshua 1:9), "Have not I commanded thee? Be strong and of a good courage," a God protecting you (as in the same place), "the Lord thy God is with thee whithersoever thou goest", and a God promising to bless and reward you. I think all this should lift up your hearts and greatly strengthen them. I read a story of one Julius Pflugius, who had been employed by the Emperor, but was much wronged and injured by the Duke of Saxony, of which complaining Caesar answered him, "Have a little patience, your cause and condition shall be my own." And this was heartening enough. God says the same to you, so make the same enlivening use of it. Weakness is strong enough if God will fight.

3. Mind the strength which you have by prayers more than the words that are against you, along with evil-minded men. The language of wicked men is but an empty breath. It may declare malice, but does not assure us of power. But the language of prayer is a mighty and doing breath; it can shake heaven and earth. The prayer of one good man has wrought wonders: it has conquered God, men, and devils. Wicked adversaries may set men to work, but prayer sets God to work. And you, right honorable, have millions of prayers almost every day sent up to

heaven for you. "It cannot be," said St. Ambrose to Monica, "that a child of so many tears and prayers should perish." So I say it cannot be that such worthies, who are every day compassed about with so many prayers, should miscarry. You have the prayers of three kingdoms for you, and I am persuaded also that you have the prayers of all the people of God throughout the whole world.

4. Mind the excellency of the issue and not the difficulty of the progress. We say in philosophy, "The end makes the work amiable and gives strength to the workman." I observe that great and choice services are more difficult when they are in agitation than when they are in action, more when we are contriving them than when we are doing them; but though they are difficult to be wrought, yet, when they are finished, they are glorious and excellent. The temple was long in building, but, when it was finished, there was nothing like it in all the world, for it was filled with the glory of the Lord from the mercy seat.

Oh, what a glory unto our good God, what a beauty to our Church, what an honor to our nation, what a satisfaction to all pious hearts, what a safety to this land, what an influence to all the churches of Christ will this reformation prove if it could be once effectually wrought by God's blessing and your successful endeavors.

Finis